AF407247

MANUSCRIPT

THE UNVARNISHED INTERIOR

NOTES FROM A LIFE EXAMINED

JACK BARUCH, MD

ISBN: 9798243171175

Cover design: Jack Baruch, MD

Interior design: Jack Baruch, MD

This book reflects the author's personal experiences, reflections, and opinions. It is not intended as psychological, medical, or legal advice.

Printed in the United States of America

EPIGRAPH

"A writer — and, I believe, all persons — must think that whatever happens to them is a resource. All things have been given to us for a purpose, and an artist must feel this more intensely. All that happens to us — including our humiliations, our misfortunes, our embarrassments — is given to us as raw material, as clay, so that we may shape our art."

— Jorge Luis Borges

"We spend our lives suspended between holding on and letting go — between the stories that shaped us and the truths that insist on being heard. Somewhere in that fragile space, we discover who we are."

— Anonymous

"If I reveal myself without worrying about how others will respond, then some will care, though others may not. But who can love me if no one knows me? I must risk it or live alone."

— Sheldon B. Kopp

DEDICATION

For my daughter, whose presence continues to give my life its deepest meaning.

For my mother, who lived 101 remarkable years, conveyed wisdom, taught me endurance, and the quiet strength of love.

For my friends, those still here, and those long gone, whose companionship shaped the contours of my life.

And for my patients, who entrusted me with their stories and, in doing so, taught me much of what appears in these pages.

PREFACE Here comes a moment in every life when the past begins to speak with a new kind of clarity — not as a collection of memories, but as a quiet insistence to be understood. When I stepped away from my psychiatric practice, I expected rest. What arrived instead was a flood of unfinished conversations: with myself, with those I had loved, with the choices I had made, and with the parts of me I had long kept at arm's length.

This book grew out of that reckoning.

The essays that follow trace the delicate thread between holding on and letting go — the lifelong negotiation between resistance and acceptance. They explore how we cling to our narratives, how we revise them, and how life revises us despite our best efforts. They examine the forces that shape our relationships, the wounds that echo across decades, the tenderness that surprises us, and the losses that carve their way into our bones.

These pages are not a linear memoir but a constellation of moments — reflections on love, aging, desire, fear, grief, and the stubborn hope that we might still grow wiser with time. They are the product of a life spent listening to patients, loved ones, and, eventually, myself.

If there is a single truth that threads through these essays, it is this: **vulnerability is not a weakness but a doorway.** It is the place where we meet ourselves most honestly, and where connection with others and with our own humanity becomes possible.

I offer these reflections not as answers, but as companions. May they meet you wherever you are on your own journey between holding on and letting go.

ADDENDUM ON WRITING THESE ESSAYS

These essays began as fragments — notes scribbled on scraps of paper, thoughts sparked by recent events, reflections that surfaced unexpectedly after decades of listening to others. When I retired from my psychiatric practice, I found myself undergoing a process not unlike psychoanalysis: sitting with my own thoughts, watching them take shape, and discovering what they revealed about the life I had lived.

Writing became a way to understand the forces that shape us — the conflicts we resist, the truths we avoid, the vulnerabilities we try to hide. Words helped me trace the threads between past and present, between the stories I had carried for years and the meanings that emerged only when I finally paused long enough to examine them.

Throughout my career, I adhered to the profession's tenets, revealing only what was necessary to further a patient's progress. Over time, I learned that selective self-disclosure — honest, measured, human — could help patients become more transparent with themselves. Except in cases of severe biochemical disorder, the difference between therapist and patient is not qualitative but quantitative. We are all navigating the same fragile terrain.

Many recoil from the word vulnerable, as if it applies only to others. But vulnerability is universal. It is the inevitable prospect of illness, limitation, loss, and life's unpredictable turns. No one escapes it. The essays that follow explore this truth from many angles — personal, professional, philosophical — and reflect my belief that acknowledging our shared humanity is not a weakness but a form of strength.

These pieces were written over thirteen years — some separated by long intervals, others composed in rapid succession. Their sequence reflects themes rather than chronology. If certain ideas recur, it is because the work of being human is recursive. We revisit the same questions, the same wounds, the same longings, until we finally understand what they have been trying to teach us.

ABOUT THE AUTHOR

I was shaped long before I understood the forces doing the shaping. I grew up as an only child in post-war New York City, raised by an immigrant mother whose love was fierce, complicated, and often overwhelming. My father was absent, my childhood accelerated by necessity, and I learned early that survival required both vigilance and imagination. I worked from a young age, not out of ambition but out of duty — a child supporting the adult who was supporting him.

Those early years carved a certain sensitivity into me, a way of listening beneath the surface of things. In retrospect, it was no surprise that I became a psychiatrist. The profession offered a language for what I had lived: the fragility of the human heart, the contradictions we carry, the longing for connection that persists despite our defenses. For forty years, I sat with people in their most unguarded moments, witnessing the quiet heroism of ordinary lives.

But my professional life did not spare me from my own complexities. I married young, hoping to create a stable family I never had, and soon became a father. Yet without role models or emotional tools, I was ill-equipped to navigate the intricacies of marriage. The relationship ended, and the years that followed were marked by several long-term partnerships and a persistent, almost phobic hesitation to remarry. That tension — between yearning and fear, closeness and retreating threads through many of the essays in this book.

I underwent years of personal psychoanalysis to better understand myself, just as I did with others. What emerged was not a single revelation but a slow, steady unearthing: the recognition that we are shaped as much by what we resist as by what we embrace. Writing became an extension of that excavation — a way to trace the emotional archaeology of my life, to make sense of the patterns that repeated themselves, and to ask how I wanted to spend the years that remained.

If there is a philosophy that underlies my work, it is this: we are all vulnerable, and we are all doing the best we can with the histories we carry. Vulnerability is not a flaw but a doorway — the place where truth enters, where connection becomes possible, where healing begins.

My life has been marked by longing, responsibility, loss, love, and the ongoing search for meaning. These essays are the distillation of that journey — reflections from a man who has lived intensely, listened deeply, failed honestly, learned slowly, and continued searching. They are offered not as answers, but as companions — an invitation to consider your own path through the fragile, resilient, bewildering condition of being human.

THE UNVARNISHED INTERIOR

Before each essay, there is a moment when something inside stirs — a discomfort, a memory, a question that refuses to stay quiet. These brief reflections are born from those moments. They are not summaries or explanations, but small windows into the impulses that shaped each piece. They offer a glimpse of the unvarnished interior from which this book was written: the raw, the unresolved, the humorous, the erotic, the grieving, the bewildered, the grateful.

Taken together, they form a kind of emotional compass — a way of orienting yourself before stepping into the deeper terrain of the essays. Read them as invitations, as quiet signals, as the first honest notes of what follows.

1. **Letting Go:** A meditation on the spiritual ideal of surrendering the invitation to release preferences, attachments, and the illusion of control. This essay asks whether true letting go is attainable or simply another aspiration we cling to in our search for peace.
2. **Capitulation:** When life overwhelms, our imagined authority dissolves. Here, I explore the strange relief found in admitting helplessness, and the unexpected strength that can emerge when we stop insisting that we can rescue every failing moment.
3. **Lamentations of an Aging Male Warrior:** A reckoning with the body's betrayals and the ego's resistance. Aging arrives like an ambush; lamentation becomes the warrior's first act of courage, clearing the way for acceptance and a renewed sense of purpose.
4. **Taking Care of the "Little Lady" — The Male Bondage:** The caretaker role can feel noble, but it can also imprison. This essay examines how duty, resentment, and fear of repetition shape a man's reluctance to risk marriage again.

5. **What Does It Mean to Be Selfish?** A dissection of the word "selfish" — who uses it, why, and what it reveals about both accuser and accused. A response to polarized reactions stirred by an earlier essay, and an attempt to understand the emotional charge behind the label.

6. **The Virtue of Tolerance:** An exploration of tolerance and intolerance as cultural forces and personal reflexes. Sometimes tolerance is grace; sometimes it is avoidance. Sometimes intolerance is cruelty; sometimes it is clarity.

7. **Living With or Without Another — Courage or Coward?** A look at the emotional architecture of solitude and partnership. The essay asks whether choosing to live alone is an act of bravery, self-protection, or something more complicated.

8. **A Time to Resist, a Time to Accept:** Life demands both defiance and surrender. This piece searches for the elusive middle ground between fighting what we cannot bear and accepting what we cannot change.

9. **Reactive Remediation:** Why do some people erupt emotionally while others absorb impact quietly? A study of reactivity — its origins, its collateral damage, and the inner work required to soften its grip.

10. **Curiosity and Its Determinants — Asset or Liability?** Curiosity can enliven or exhaust, attract or repel. This essay explores why some people are endlessly inquisitive while others remain self-contained — and how each stance shapes intimacy.

11. **Criteria and Beyond in the Pursuit of a Relationship:** We cling to "criteria" when choosing a partner, but do they guide us or mislead us? A reflection on how checklists can obscure deeper truths about desire, fear, and readiness.

12. **Our Narrative — Honest or Not?** We all carry a story about who we were and who we've become. This essay confronts the resistance to updating that story — and the liberation that comes when we finally do.

13. **Now What?** After achieving what we thought we wanted, a strange emptiness can follow. This piece asks whether

fulfillment is finite or whether there is always another layer waiting to be uncovered.

14. **Remedial Gratitude:** A companion to "Now What?", this essay challenges the belief that "having everything" ends the search. It argues that gratitude is not a conclusion but a practice that expands what we think is possible.

15. **Stuff and the Search for Simplicity:** A meditation on the objects we accumulate and the psychic weight they carry. Letting go of possessions becomes a metaphor for releasing the deeper burdens we've carried for far longer.

16. **Being a Psychiatrist:** A personal account of what drew me into psychiatry and what it has taken from and given to me. A life spent listening — and the toll and privilege of that vocation.

17. **Getting Back in the Driver's Seat:** Two simple but powerful shifts in thinking that restore agency when life feels unmanageable. A reminder that control often begins with the stories we tell ourselves.

18. **Something in Return:** How parents shape entitlement, gratitude, and resilience in their children. An exploration of the subtle ways love can nourish growth — or quietly stunt it.

19. **Seven Words That Kill a Relationship:** A moment with a golf partner becomes a lesson in emotional responsibility. This essay looks at how a single reflexive phrase can shut down connection — and what a healthier alternative might be.

20. **You Can't Please or Displease Anyone Ever:** A reframing of how we interpret others' reactions to us. The essay places emotional ownership back where it belongs and frees us from the exhausting task of managing other people's feelings.

21. **Let It Be:** A meditation on non-reactivity — the art of observing without absorbing. A call to cultivate the inner stillness that allows life to unfold without constant interference.

22. **Swaggering Mortality:** Childhood wounds echo into adulthood, shaping our instinctive responses to strangers. This piece explores how early triggers distort perception and how compassion can soften those reflexes.

23. **Hopelessly Living in Hope:** A look at the despair that arises when we cling to the fantasy that a hopeless situation will magically improve. A study of the emotional cost of refusing to accept reality.

24. **Multiple Relationships with One Person — A Preventive Antidote to Infidelity:** An exploration of the psychological roots of infidelity and a proposal for a surprising antidote: cultivating multiple dimensions of connection with the same partner rather than seeking them elsewhere.

25. **On Infidelity:** A broader, deeper examination of the forces that drive or prevent betrayal. This essay expands the conversation, exploring monogamy, desire, and the complex terrain of human attachment.

26. **Protect Them from Suicide:** Inspired by a filmmaker who documented Golden Gate Bridge jumpers, this essay reflects on our moral responsibility to intervene when someone is spiraling toward self-destruction — even in subtle, everyday ways.

27. **My Ballerina:** A deeply personal portrait of a relationship with a gifted dancer whose brilliance is shadowed by an eating disorder. A study of love, frustration, admiration, and the limits of rescue.

28. **The Lure of the Vulnerable Woman:** A candid exploration of the magnetic pull of vulnerability — how it captivates, how it misleads, and how it often echoes unresolved childhood wounds. A search for healthier forms of attraction.

29. **Predatory Men and Their Just Desserts:** A frank look at male sexual instinct, cultural conditioning, and the consequences that inevitably follow. A stark commentary on desire, entitlement, and the shifting landscape of gender dynamics.

30. **A Strange Reunion:** A reunion with a long-ago love, made possible by social media, becomes a meditation on memory, longing, and the impossibility of recreating the past. A brief, exquisite encounter that illuminates why some relationships remain unfinished in the heart.

31. **Reuniting With the Past:** A series of reconnections with former loves reveals how time sharpens discernment. What once felt negotiable no longer is; with fewer years ahead, the quality of connection becomes non-negotiable.

32. **Becoming Physically Intimate — Sooner or Later?** An exploration of how timing shapes intimacy. Whether we move quickly or slowly, each pace carries its own risks, revelations, and emotional consequences.

33. **Regrettably Out of Sync:** A rare experience of limerence becomes a study in longing, timing, and the intoxicating pull of possibility. The essay examines what happens when two people ignite — but not at the same moment.

34. **Older Men with Younger Women:** A candid look at the dynamics that draw older men to younger women — and vice versa. The essay probes the psychological undercurrents, the illusions, and the realities that determine whether such relationships endure.

35. **Confusion and Diminished Sexual Power:** A frank reflection on the unsettling shift men experience when the lifelong pursuit of women loses its urgency. The essay examines what fades, what remains, and what new identity must be forged in the aftermath.

36. **Duplicity:** A story of charm, deception, and emotional ambush. This essay traces an encounter that dazzled, disarmed, and ultimately devastated — a mystery that still resists resolution.

37. **Closing the Deal:** A personal account of wrestling with the decision to commit fully to one woman. The essay unpacks the competing desires, fears, and internal negotiations that determine whether a relationship becomes a life.

38. **My Mother Approaches 100:** A tribute to my mother as she is near a century of life. This piece reflects our complicated bond, the softening that comes with time, and the urgency of creating a meaningful final chapter together.

39. **My Mother's Protector:** A deeply personal exploration of the lifelong responsibility I carried as my mother's primary caretaker. The essay examines the emotional cost, the unspoken

dynamics, and the growth that emerged from a role I never chose but fully inhabited.

40. **Going Gently into the Night:** A tender account of my mother's final days — a departure marked by clarity, grace, and mutual permission. A meditation on beauty that can accompany a conscious, peaceful goodbye.

41. **Mother's Death — A Giant Void:** In the wake of her passing, grief collides with an unexpected sense of freedom. This essay explores the disorientation of losing both a mother and a lifelong role.

42. **Farewell to a Good Friend:** A letter written to a dying friend becomes a reminder to tell our truths while there is still time. A meditation on love, mortality, and the urgency of saying what matters.

43. **Death and Its Impact:** A year marked by multiple losses forces a reckoning with mortality and the shrinking circle of one's world. The essay considers how grief reshapes priorities and accelerates change.

44. **A New State of Mind:** After a cascade of losses, solitude becomes not an escape but a preference. This piece explores the desire to simplify, to prune relationships, and to devote one's remaining time to what feels essential.

45. **Vulnerable Breakthrough:** A rare moment of emotional nakedness reveals the child within — unguarded, unfiltered, and profoundly alive. The essay honors the transformative power of vulnerability when defenses finally fall away.

46. **A Harrowing Month:** A misdiagnosis with fatal implications shatters trust in medical authority and forces a confrontation with vulnerability. The essay traces the emotional debris left behind when certainty collapses.

47. **Satisfaction:** An inquiry into what satisfaction means when chronic pain shadows daily life. A meditation on how contentment must sometimes be redefined rather than pursued.

48. **Regained Simplicity:** After decades of responsibility, a quieter life emerges — unstructured, uncluttered, and unexpectedly

nourishing. This essay honors the grace of simplicity and the gratitude it invites.

49. **A Break into the Void:** A reflection on the creative emptiness that precedes expression. The essay explores how something — anything — is coaxed out of nothing, and how the void itself becomes part of the process.

50. **Raging Over Bad Luck:** Why do trivial misfortunes provoke such disproportionate fury? A look at the deeper meanings we attach to randomness and the emotional residue that small losses stir up.

51. **The Meaning of Winning and Losing:** Winning and losing are rarely about the score. This essay examines the fragile egos, cultural pressures, and existential stakes that turn competition into a metaphor for self-worth.

52. **Aborted Vacation:** A disastrous attempt to reach the Swiss Alps becomes a study in frustration, resilience, and the emotional cost of navigating incompetence. A reminder that even leisure can test us.

53. **Reflective Transitions on Coming Home:** Returning to the place of childhood after a lifetime away prompts a reckoning with identity, retirement, and the challenge of filling newly open time. A meditation on circling back.

54. **Golf as a Metaphor on Character:** Golf becomes a lens through which character reveals itself — patience, ego, resilience, self-deception. The essay explores what this maddening game teaches about life.

55. **Integrity at Its Best:** A brief, almost surreal encounter on a bike ride in Nantucket becomes a testament to unexpected morality. A reminder that integrity often appears quietly, without announcement.

56. **My Best Friend — What Does That Mean?** A reflection on the qualities that define a best friend and a tribute to the people who have held that role in my life. An exploration of loyalty, history, and emotional refuge.

57. **The Origin of a Hobby — Truth or Fiction?** A playful inquiry into the mysterious roots of my fascination with African

antiquities, Afro-Cuban music, conga drumming, and dance. A speculative journey into the origins of passion.

58. **Once Upon a Mambo:** A light, affectionate reminiscence of my years immersed in mambo dancing — the music, the mentors, the joy. A celebration of rhythm as a form of identity.

59. **"You Ain't Nobody."** A late-life reckoning with identity, mortality, and the fragile narratives that sustain us. It asks: Who am I when everything is stripped away?

60. **Being Understood — The Ultimate Aphrodisiac:** An exploration of the profound relief and intimacy that arise when someone truly understands us — and the loneliness that follows when they don't. A meditation on connection as the deepest form of desire.

Unified Introduction to Thematic Architecture

A life is not lived in straight lines. It unfolds in cycles — resistance and acceptance, longing and loss, intimacy and solitude, ambition and surrender. These essays trace those cycles with honesty and precision, moving from the private interior world to the charged spaces of relationships, desire, memory, family, work, and, finally, the quiet reckoning of later life.

The book is organized not by chronology but by **psychological terrain**. Each section marks a different facet of the human journey: the struggle to live with oneself, the challenge of living with others, the mysteries of desire, the return of the past, the weight of family, and the freedom that emerges when obligation falls away. Together, they form a map — not of answers, but of the questions that shape a life.

THEMATIC GROUPING

SECTION I — The Work of Being Human

(Foundations: Resistance, Acceptance, Identity, and Meaning)

Essays:

- Letting Go
- Capitulation
- Lamentations of an Aging Male Warrior
- A Time to Resist, a Time to Accept
- Now What
- Remedial Gratitude
- Stuff and the Search for Simplicity
- Regained Simplicity
- A Break into the Void
- Raging Over Bad Luck

- The Meaning of Winning and Losing
- Aborted Vacation
- Reflective Transitions on Coming Home
- Satisfaction

Why this grouping works

These essays explore the lifelong tension between resisting reality and learning to inhabit it with clarity and grace. They form the emotional and philosophical foundation of the book.

SECTION II — The Self in Relationship

(Emotional Patterns, Communication, and Personal Growth)

Essays:

- What Does It Mean to Be Selfish?
- The Virtue of Tolerance
- Living With or Without Another — Courage or Coward?
- Criteria and Beyond in the Pursuit of a Relationship
- Our Narrative — Honest or Not?
- Getting Back in the Driver's Seat
- Reactive Remediation
- Curiosity and Its Determinants — Asset or Liability?
- Seven Words That Kill a Relationship
- You Can't Please or Displease Anyone Ever
- Let It Be
- Being Understood — The Ultimate Aphrodisiac

Why this grouping works

These essays illuminate the emotional patterns that shape how we relate to others — the reflexes we inherit, the stories we cling to, and the blind spots that quietly sabotage connection. Together, they reveal that intimacy is less about choosing the right partner and more about understanding the self we bring into every encounter. This section serves as the psychological bridge between inner and relational life, showing how growth begins with self-awareness.

SECTION III — Love, Desire, and the Erotic Mind

(Intimacy, Attraction, Timing, and Sexual Psychology)

Essays:

- Taking Care of the "Little Lady" — The Male Bondage
- Multiple Relationships with One Person — A Preventive Antidote to Infidelity
- On Infidelity
- Becoming Physically Intimate — Sooner or Later?
- Regrettably Out of Sync
- Older Men with Younger Women
- Confusion and Diminished Sexual Power
- Duplicity
- Closing the Deal
- The Lure of the Vulnerable Woman
- Predatory Men and Their Just Desserts

Why this grouping works

These essays explore the charged terrain of desire — its timing, its distortions, its vulnerabilities, and its lifelong evolution. They examine the unconscious forces that pull us toward certain people and away from others, revealing how sexuality is inseparable from history, fantasy, and fear. This section deepens the emotional arc of the book by showing how longing exposes our most tender truths and unresolved wounds.

SECTION IV — Encounters, Echoes, and the Past Returning

(Memory, Unfinished Stories, and the People Who Return)

Essays:

- A Strange Reunion
- Reuniting With the Past
- My Ballerina
- Vulnerable Breakthrough

Why this grouping works

These essays trace the quiet power of memory and the unfinished stories that resurface when we least expect them. They reveal how past relationships continue to shape identity, desire, and self-understanding long after they've ended. This section serves as a reflective pause in the manuscript — a space where the reader confronts the echoes of earlier selves and the emotional residue that time never fully erases.

SECTION V — Family, Caregiving, and the Weight of Legacy

(Parents, Mortality, Responsibility, and Transformation)

Essays:

- Something in Return
- My Mother Approaches 100
- My Mother's Protector
- Going Gently into the Night

- Mother's Death — A Giant Void
- Farewell to a Good Friend
- Death and Its Impact
- A New State of Mind
- A Harrowing Month
- Protect Them from Suicide

Why this grouping works

These essays anchor the book in its deepest emotional territory: the responsibilities we inherit, the roles we never chose, and the transformations that follow loss. They explore caregiving, mortality, devotion, exhaustion, and the profound reshaping of identity that occurs when a parent declines and dies. This section forms the emotional core of the manuscript, revealing how love and grief carve the contours of a life.

SECTION VI — Work, Friendship, and Life Beyond Obligation

(Character, Freedom, Aging, and the Final Reckonings)

Essays:

- Being a psychiatrist
- Golf as a Metaphor on Character
- Integrity at Its Best
- My Best Friend — What Does That Mean?
- The Origin of a Hobby — Truth or Fiction?
- Once Upon a Mambo
- Swaggering Mortality
- Hopelessly Living in Hope
- You Ain't Nobody

Why this grouping works

These essays explore the self that emerges when striving, proving, and performing finally loosen their grip. They examine character, friendship, curiosity, rhythm, and the unexpected freedoms of later life. As the book moves toward its final reckoning, these pieces reveal what remains when external roles fall away — the distilled self, shaped by choice rather than obligation. This section prepares the reader for the manuscript's closing movement, where identity is stripped to its essentials.

TABLE OF CONTENTS

SECTION I — The Work of Being Human

SECTION II — The Self in Relationship

SECTION III — Love, Desire, and the Erotic Mind

LETTING GO

"The Great Way is not difficult for those who have no preferences. When love and hate are both absent, everything becomes clear and undisguised. Make the smallest distinction, however, and heaven and earth are set infinitely apart. If you wish to see the truth, then hold no opinion for or against it. The struggle of what one likes and what one dislikes is the disease of the mind." — Hsin Hsin Ming: The Book of Nothing

A central theme running through my life—and through this collection of essays—is the struggle to surrender to what is. Letting things be, without forcing them into the shape of my preferences, has always felt like an elusive ideal. The impulse to direct, control, influence, or engineer a particular outcome is deeply ingrained. Sometimes it yields the illusion of success, but often it exacts a toll on the mind and body that far outweighs whatever victory we imagine we've achieved.

The desire to detach from this relentless striving is so pervasive precisely because the human condition is so acquisitive. From infancy onward, we want what we want, when we want it. When we get it, we feel a fleeting sense of mastery; when we don't, we feel vulnerable, frustrated, or distressed. As we age, we may disguise these reactions under a veneer of maturity or serenity, but beneath the surface, the emotional twitch remains. We still want things to turn out a certain way. We still resist what is.

Is it realistic to aspire to the Eastern ideal of giving up preferences altogether? The notion sounds noble: accept everything simply because it happens. But when something occurs that we do not want, the mind rebels. Sustained resistance becomes a recipe for chronic distress, even madness. And yet, the alternative—radical acceptance—can feel equally impossible. Still, if peace of mind is a priority, the effort seems worth making.

Where does this resistance come from? Is it hardwired into our biology, a survival mechanism that pushes us to win, to control, to shape our environment? Or is it learned—a product of a competitive culture that rewards achievement and punishes failure? Perhaps it's a mixture of both: genetic predispositions, prenatal influences, early experiences, and the social pressures that mold us from childhood onward.

Spiritual teachers across traditions urge us to let go, to relinquish attachment to outcomes, to stay present. Yet the drive to succeed, to shape events, to impose our will persists. Like Sisyphus, we push the boulder up the mountain each day, only to watch it roll back down. The struggle gives structure to our lives, even meaning. Writing this essay, for example, fills the void with purpose. Meanwhile, the meditative emptiness of simply being—though peaceful—rarely feels sufficient on its own.

Life continually presents new goals: work, love, health, mastery, dignity. When any of these falters, a restless sense of incompletion arises. Does it ever end? Do we ever reach a point where we can say, "I've done enough; now I can let go"? Or do we struggle until the very end, clinging to the simplest of goals—getting out of bed without falling, preparing our meals, maintaining a measure of independence?

Eventually, health breaks down. Resistance flares. Acceptance becomes difficult. I often wonder about those who seem naturally able to roll with life's punches. How much of that ease is genetic? I once watched an interview with a professional golfer who said he had always been calm, even as a child. No matter the shot, he never became upset. I thought, "Lucky man—he was born with the tranquility gene." The rest of us must work at it, often with mixed results.

Life has its own plans, indifferent to our preferences. Who wants to work that hard trying to control it? Better to give our best input, then move on. I was reminded of this when I volunteered to call every member of my medical school class for our 50th reunion. Some conversations were pleasant; others were filled with decades of bitterness. One woman, quiet throughout medical school, snapped, "It's none of your damn business," when I asked why she couldn't attend. Her hostility stunned me. After fifty years, this was her voice emerging at last. I wished her well and let it go.

Letting go is a process shaped by life's circumstances and by deliberate discipline. It means allowing things to unfold without forcing them into our preferred mold. In love, especially, disappointment arises from unmet expectations—preferences dressed up as hopes. Without preferences, disappointment would vanish. In theory, we could love everyone as they are. Most people can't achieve that degree of spiritual idealism.

Are there people who can truly extinguish preferences and live in equanimity, untouched by sadness, anger, fear, or even joy? Perhaps only those who devote their lives to spiritual practice—monks, ascetics, mystics—come close. They are fed, housed, and freed from worldly concerns, allowing them to embrace "The Great Way," the path of non-resistance. For the rest of us, survival demands preferences. We cannot simply float through life without them.

Maybe I've misunderstood Hsin Hsin Ming's teaching. Perhaps he does not mean we should eliminate our emotional reactions, but rather that we should not resist them. If we are angry, let the anger be. If we are sad, let the sadness be. Observe the emotion without demanding it be different. Want nothing more than what is already present. No preference for another state. No struggle. Just awareness.

It may be the closest we can come to letting go.

Addendum: As The Beatles sang: *"Let it be, let it be. Whisper words of wisdom, let it be."*

CAPITULATION

"Success is not final; failure is not fatal. It is the courage to continue that counts." — Winston Churchill.

I have spent much of my life trying to surrender to what is — to stop resisting, to stop insisting that life conforms to my preferences, to stop believing that sheer willpower can bend reality to my liking. At times, I've tasted a fraction of serenity, a fleeting sense of peace. But just as quickly, life delivers another blow: an unexpected event, a sudden loss, a shift so jarring it flings me into helplessness. The cycle repeats — calm, disruption, adaptation — as if the universe were reminding me that control is, at best, a temporary illusion.

Some people seem to glide through life with fewer disruptions, buoyed by luck, health, and a sense of mastery. They work, play, love, and parent with the quiet confidence that things will generally go their way. When setbacks occur, they recover quickly, restoring equilibrium with minimal turbulence. But for many of us, life unfolds differently. One thing goes wrong, then another, and another still. Each time, we believe we can fix it, stave off adversity, or muscle our way back to stability. Sometimes we succeed. Other times, the rug is pulled out from beneath us, and no amount of effort can stop the bleeding.

In youth, we believe we are omnipotent. We imagine we can control our destiny through sheer determination. That illusion is necessary; it gives us the confidence to venture into the world. But for some, early trauma or abusive environments crush that belief before it can take root. A child whose spirit is broken grows into an adult who doubts his ability to navigate life's rough waters. Others, raised without limits, may become superstars — or face a rude awakening when they discover that mastery is never guaranteed.

Wherever we fall on that developmental continuum, the truth remains: succeeding in school, work, relationships, health, and personal growth rarely comes naturally. It requires effort, persistence, and resilience.

We study, we practice, we take lessons, we exercise, we eat well, we follow the advice of experts — financial advisors, physicians, teachers, therapists — believing that if we do everything "right," life will reward us. And yet, even when we follow the rules, we may still run into a wall.

How perplexing, how maddening, to discover that the so-called experts are often no more certain than we are. Their clay feet flop around just like ours. They project confidence, but their predictions are educated guesses at best. As children, we believed adults knew everything. As adults, we discover that no one truly does.

I remember the air-raid drills in New York City during World War II. As a young child, I sat on my mother's lap in the dark, shades drawn, sirens blaring. She whispered, "It's alright, Jackie, everything will be fine." Her reassurance soothed me, and I believed her completely. How comforting it was to feel protected. How illusory that protection turned out to be.

Eventually, we grow older and realize there is no one left to reassure us. We become self-reliant, navigating ambiguity with whatever tools we've acquired. We crave clarity, yet life offers nebulosity. To cope, we construct temporary certainties — beliefs, routines, explanations — that hold us together just long enough to move forward.

As a psychiatrist, I was one of those "experts" people turned to for answers. I offered guidance, probability, insight — but rarely certainty. Even the most brilliant professional's blunder. Presidents, Federal Reserve chairmen, physicians, attorneys, financial advisors, teachers — all make mistakes. And when they do, the consequences can be irreversible for those who trust them.

When catastrophe strikes, the urge to quit, run, or self-destruct can be overwhelming. Some succumb. Most cling desperately to hope, believing things will improve. A skilled professional must walk a delicate line: conveying difficult truths while preserving enough hope to keep someone going.

Complete capitulation — true surrender — is terrifying. It occurs when we have no choice but to yield to forces far greater than ourselves. Fortunately, such moments are rare. Preparing for them is nearly impossible unless one has spent years cultivating a monk-like discipline, learning to accept the unacceptable with a measure of peace. For most of us, the ego resists until the very end.

Consider the prisoner on death row, the hostage awaiting execution, the terminal patient receiving devastating news. Up until the final moment, they cling to hope — a reprieve, a rescue, a miracle. In those moments, we regress to childhood, calling upon parents or God to save us. When no rescue comes, surrender arrives. And paradoxically, with total capitulation, peace sometimes follows. At best, we accept the irreversible. At worst, we remain trapped in anguish until the end.

Addendum: Nietzsche wrote, "That which does not kill us makes us stronger." Life's narrow escapes, frightening diagnoses, misdiagnoses, and losses are devastating, yet they shape us. The unseen benefit is the strength, wisdom, and meaning that emerge on the other side. Gratitude becomes a mantra: thank you, thank you… Thank you — not for the suffering, but for the fact that we survived it without having to capitulate entirely.

LAMENTATIONS OF AN AGING MALE WARRIOR

*"Fight on, my men," says Sir Andrew Barton, *"I am hurt, but I am not slain. I'll lie me down and bleed awhile, and then I'll rise and fight again. "*— Thomas Moore

It creeps up slowly, almost imperceptibly, and then one day the realization hits with a force that leaves you breathless: you've lost your edge. That mysterious combination of vitality, confidence, and magnetism — the *je ne sais quoi* that once defined you — has begun to fade. You sense it before anyone says a word. The looks linger less. The energy shifts. People no longer see you; they look past you, through you, as if some essential spark has dimmed.

You ask yourself. *"What happened? Where did my power go? My leverage? My manhood?"* Did it slip away quietly while I wasn't paying attention? Or did I set myself up for this vulnerability by avoiding remarriage, failing to insulate myself from the inevitable dismissal from the gene pool?

For much of my life, athletic prowess was part of my identity — a symbolic badge of the warrior. I skied black diamonds, telemarked through deep powder, played fast singles tennis, hit hard serves and overheads, and ran marathons with times I was proud of. Then came the first knee surgery. Then the failed lumbar surgery. Then the second knee surgery. Goodbye tennis. Goodbye running. Goodbye skiing. The body that once obeyed now resists, and the warrior's armor begins to crack.

Life's illusions are fragile. The fickle finger of fate pokes its head around the corner and whispers, "Lose the illusions before your teeth." And then, as if to drive the point home, a more serious medical blow arrives. Prostate cancer. A diagnosis that shakes any man to his core. Even if caught early, the treatment can alter one's sexual identity overnight. For eighteen months, erectile power diminished, along with confidence, swagger, and the easy optimism that once came naturally.

I found myself shrinking, tail between my legs, avoiding women out of fear and shame.

It's astonishing how much of our identity — consciously or not — becomes tied to sexual capacity. Slowly, painfully, through months of penile injections and the eventual help of Viagra, some semblance of function returned. But the fear of recurrence lingered. And then came another blow: two episodes of paroxysmal atrial fibrillation, likely triggered by too much wine. Hours in the emergency room, heart racing unpredictably, left me shaken. As a physician, I knew too much. Whatever vestiges of invincibility remained slipped away.

I stopped drinking alcohol. Stopped caffeine. Ate healthier. Took supplements. Tried to stabilize my cardiac system. My values shifted. Investments, material acquisitions, fancy cars, clothes, gadgets — all of it felt trivial. Survival and quality of life became the only currencies that mattered.

I tried returning to the slopes. The muscle memory was there, but the knee buckled, swelled, and reminded me that skiing was no longer a place of joy but of risk. Tennis felt constrained, stripped of the fluidity I once loved. Running became walking. Each attempt to reclaim the past only highlighted the distance between who I was and who I had become.

Memory can be cruel. It kept yesterday alive with such clarity that today feels like a betrayal. The cognitive dissonance is relentless: the mind remembers the warrior; the body refuses to comply. Viagra helps, yes — but I would trade the pill for my pre-surgical body in a heartbeat. That fantasy, however, is off the table.

Still, gratitude is essential. Many men never regain sexual function after prostate surgery. Many face far worse outcomes. I remind myself of this often. I remind myself that catching cancer early was a blessing, even if the shadow of recurrence never fully disappears.

In my younger years, I defined myself — unconsciously, perhaps — through achievement: athletic, academic, romantic. I succeeded in all three. Then I retired from a profession I loved, still at the top of my game, only to be met with a succession of bodily assaults that stripped away the arenas where I once excelled. Pride plummeted. Identity wavered. The warrior felt unarmed.

But grief cannot be a permanent home. At some point, I must redefine myself, change the internal conversation, and create a new possibility rather than clinging to the man I once was. Perhaps writing — using my intellect, my insight, my lived experience — can become a new arena, one that offers meaning without requiring physical prowess.

Life ebbs and flows. We have it, then lose it, then regain some portion of it, then lose again. A wounded warrior may lament, but eventually he stands, dusts himself off, and begins anew. This time, the beginning is not a return to what was, but a discovery of what has never been. The battles ahead are different, but no less worthy.

Whether we like it or not, the warrior persists. The lamentations are part of the journey — sometimes silent, sometimes spoken, always deeply felt. Few of us make it through life unscathed. It takes courage, emotional skill, and resilience to endure the inevitable losses and heartbreaks. Emerging with dignity is a victory.

Addendum: I write to work through the pain, much as I did in the psychoanalytic work I both gave and received over the years. Putting thoughts and feelings on the page, reading them, revisiting them, reflecting on them — this keeps me on the road toward healthier choices. Writing has become both a mirror and a companion, guiding me toward whatever comes next.

TAKING CARE OF THE "LITTLE LADY" —— THE MALE BONDAGE

"Death tugs at my ear and says, Live. I am coming." — Oliver Wendell Holmes, Sr.

It has never given me any thrill, pride, or sense of importance to know that men of my generation were raised to be caretakers of the so-called "little lady." That was the script handed to us from childhood: open the door, give up your seat, protect her at all costs, and if necessary, sacrifice your life. Women and children first. The man goes down with the ship. Embedded in that chivalrous doctrine was a quiet assumption — that women were fragile, dependent, and in need of male protection. A residue of an earlier era, yes, but one that persisted well into my adulthood.

Many men of my generation bought into it wholeheartedly. They worked themselves to the bone to support their wives and children, often at the expense of their own health. Meanwhile, the traditional woman played tennis or mahjong at the country club while the nanny or maid tended to the household. Others, with fewer financial resources, stayed home and did the hard, undervalued labor of raising children and maintaining a home — a full-time job that deserved far more respect than it received.

Before I reached the point of no return, I took flight from my marriage for reasons irrelevant here, and in its place paid the alimony fine. The courts ensured that the "little lady" maintained her accustomed lifestyle. I know the term is demeaning — and I'm not proud of the residual anger that still seeps out when I use it — but it reflects the emotional truth of that period in my life.

I watched friends and colleagues remain in their marriages, working tirelessly to uphold that lifestyle. Some even took pride in it, flaunting their wives' diamond rings, fur coats, and new convertibles as badges of success. I found it deplorable, the antithesis of everything I aspired to be. Yet I also understood that for some men, providing that lifestyle was an expression of love, commitment, and gratitude — not just obligation or unconscious modeling after their fathers.

After my divorce, I chose a different path. I cooked, cleaned, did my laundry, managed my household, and arranged my social life. I wrote my own checks. I also did the legwork required to satisfy my sexual needs. Over the years, I had several long-term, meaningful relationships — loving, mutually supportive partnerships that offered security without the legal entanglements of marriage. Still, I sometimes wonder whether I deceived myself, rationalizing a life built around independence and self-protection.

My divorce came when I was a young medical resident earning $500 a month. I paid my wife $450 of it. That left me $50 to live on. I survived by moonlighting — delivering babies, working in emergency rooms — all while enduring the grueling demands of residency. The bitterness lingered. I paid alimony for thirty-eight years. Supporting my daughter was a joy; supporting my ex-wife was something else entirely.

As I dated in the years that followed, I became attuned to red flags. I once took a woman to several restaurants, and she never once reached for the check. Not even at the movies did she offer to buy the tickets. That degree of entitlement propelled me straight to the exit.

Yet I also took many women on lavish vacations and fine dining experiences — women who could not have afforded such luxuries. Their pleasure was mine. But when a woman with substantial means expected me to foot the bill simply because I was the man, I found it intolerable.

I remember being fixed up with a wealthy divorcée — Fifth Avenue apartment, homes in Palm Springs and Beverly Hills. She made a reservation at an upscale restaurant. When the check came, she excused herself to the restroom. I paid. The next night, she proudly announced she had secured a table at Le Cirque. "Who do you think will pay for that meal?" I asked. "The gentleman, of course," she replied. "Not this gentleman," I said. She was stunned — but agreed. Still, her scornful laughter about the alimony she received despite her wealth was enough to turn me away.

Perhaps I should be more tolerant. Some women measure their worth by how much a man indulges them. They believe they must be more treasured, more desirable, if a man pays, supports, and takes care of them. Others believe offering to pay insults the man's masculinity. These rationalizations are deeply ingrained, culturally sanctioned, and emotionally complex.

But they still rub me the wrong way.

Feminists, on the other hand, refuse to be beholden. They insist on paying for themselves — and sometimes for their men. I find that refreshing, not threatening.

As for sexual "goodies," I've always felt that men offer something just as valuable as women do. Why should one be treated as a premium commodity and the other as a given? Perhaps this dynamic evolved as a protective adaptation — a way for women to control men's testosterone-driven impulses and secure commitment. Religion and social norms reinforced it, making women appear passive while men pursued, pleaded, and paid for access to intimacy.

Somewhere along the way, I drifted from my original question: how to resolve my conflict about taking care of the "little lady" and the burden it creates. The answer may lie in accepting the price of partnership without obsessing over fairness. What does it take to feel the deal is reasonable? What must I receive in return to give freely without resentment?

Sex alone is not enough. I've been there. I've done that. At this stage of life, something deeper matters: true love, emotional safety, reliability, integrity, companionship, laughter, vulnerability, shared curiosity, and mutual desire. If I found a woman who embodied these qualities, the cost-benefit analysis would dissolve. The resentment would evaporate. The role of caretaker would feel natural, even joyful.

But I am in the warm September of my years. How much time remains to find such a person? Perhaps my ideal — bright, witty, sensual, financially independent, unencumbered, available to travel and play — is unrealistic. A pipe dream. No one gets everything. Something will always be missing.

Still, I am not the same man I was decades ago. Perhaps I could attract a woman aligned with who I've become. If I found such a partner, I suspect the cynical conversation about "taking care of the little lady" would vanish. Age softens us. We become more appreciative, less perfectionistic, and more accepting of human limitations. We recognize that we cannot have it all.

In the past, the price felt too high for the return. But even the independent woman who "has it all" is far from free. The question is whether the cost is worth the life shared.

Addendum: I am trying to understand the impediments that have kept me from surrendering to a lasting, loving relationship. My childhood — an only child of divorce, burdened with responsibility, exposed to volatility — shaped my need for independence and my aversion to emotional entanglement. Early self-reliance becomes a comfort zone that is hard to relinquish. If I eventually find myself happily partnered, I will know I created that possibility. If not, perhaps I was fooling myself — or perhaps the scars ran deeper than I realized. Or maybe, just maybe, Lady Luck simply wasn't with me.

WHAT DOES IT MEAN TO BE SELFISH?

"If I am not for myself, who will be for me? If I am not for others, what am I? And if not now, when? — Rabbi Hillel, Jewish scholar & theologian (30 BC – 9 AD)

I often wonder whether my reflective writing is a sincere attempt to teach and learn, or whether it veers into narcissistic self-absorption. After forty years in psychiatry, surrounded by colleagues and patients who examined their conscious and unconscious motivations with relentless scrutiny, self-reflection became second nature. It was a moral imperative — part of the indoctrination of becoming a psychiatrist — to remain alert to the subtleties of one's psyche lest we inadvertently wreak havoc on the minds of others.

So, it felt natural to continue this introspective habit after retiring to Key Biscayne. The weather is beautiful, the air clean, the pace relaxed — ideal for golf, tennis, sailing, or fishing. But tranquility can come at a cost. In seeking refuge from the intensity of my professional life, I may have over-idealized peace and underestimated the intellectual and psychological landscape of my new environment.

From my high-rise condominium, with the ocean on one side and Biscayne Bay on the other, the view is magnificent. But the exit toll — the loss of intellectual stimulation and psychological sophistication I once took for granted — became increasingly apparent. Manhattan and Washington, D.C., where I lived and practiced for decades, offered a level of curiosity and depth that Southern Florida rarely matches. In the land of the blind, the one-eyed man may be king, but the king is often lonely.

Hoping for meaningful feedback, I began reading my essays aloud to others. My professional friends and those familiar with therapy responded thoughtfully. But reading to a group of lay residents in my upscale community was another matter entirely. Many seemed pleasant enough — from the Midwest, New England, Canada, South America, Europe, South Africa, and a sprinkling of New Yorkers —

but few understood the process I was engaged in. I began to suspect that the audience for deeply personal, psychologically nuanced essays might be smaller than I imagined.

In cosmopolitan cities, one becomes insulated, forgetting that most people do not spend their lives pondering the human condition. Many see the world in black-and-white terms, with little appetite for emotional nuance. To them, my essays — filled with introspection and self-disclosure — may appear like a self-indulgent feast drenched in egotistical gravy.

At a recent reading, a woman responded to a vulnerable essay by saying, "It seems to me that you think too much. Can't you just accept things at face value?" I asked whether she believed it best to let sleeping dogs lie. "Oh, no!" she replied, missing the irony entirely. I considered quoting Socrates as "The unexamined life is not worth living" — but sensed it would only deepen her bewilderment. Later, she added, "Doctor, your basic problem is that you're selfish." When I asked her to define selfish, she snapped, "You know exactly what I mean!"

I resisted the urge to react. Sensitivity, fortunately, trumped grandiosity.

Another man offered a similar critique, though he could not articulate why. His tone was swaggeringly self-righteous, reminiscent of patients who projected unresolved conflicts onto others. When I attempted to discuss the value of self-examination, he declared, "I have no desire to examine my inner self and never will." His conviction struck me as defensive — a shield against the terror of discovering he had lived a long life devoid of curiosity.

I reminded myself that offering unsolicited insight outside the office can provoke defensiveness. After all, who wants to admit to being unaware of themselves? Retirement has its downsides; I miss the respect and gratitude of patients who sought my guidance. Out in the real world, I sometimes feel like Rodney Dangerfield — no respect at all.

Still, my own selfishness surfaced when I confronted the man. His smugness triggered my countertransference. I rationalized the confrontation as therapeutic, but in truth, it was a justification to avoid examining my own irritation. My desire to retaliate was the residue of a selfish child, not the compassion of a seasoned psychiatrist.

Does anyone ever become so evolved, so grounded in love and compassion, that no matter how others behave, love prevails? I will never be Mother Teresa. My mental ecology rebels against such vulnerability. As a psychiatrist, I used my reaction or countertransference as a tool — a way to understand how patients interacted with the world. But outside the consulting room, that same reactivity can be a liability.

I've noticed that those who accuse others of selfishness are often deeply self-centered themselves. Limited in empathy, they cannot step into another's experience. True empathy requires dissolving the self long enough to inhabit another's emotional space. A genuinely caring person knows how to say the right words to make someone feel acknowledged rather than rebuked.

Reading personal essays to strangers carries inherent risk. After one such evening, I wondered whether I was, in fact, selfish. So, I began examining the possibility.

To determine whether I am selfish, I must evaluate my acts of giving and ask whether they were rooted in compassion or self-interest. I must also consider the origins of selfishness — an innate characteristic present from birth, gradually tempered by discipline, loving role models, religious teachings, and therapeutic work. All children are inherently self-centered; over time, they learn to consider others' needs. Yet here I am, a well-trained psychiatrist, still struggling at times to keep my opinions to myself, especially with those I love.

Should we refrain from giving unsolicited advice to our children? Or is it more loving to intervene when we see them making painful mistakes? I find it difficult to remain silent when I sense trouble. My experience gives me a nose for danger they have not yet developed. Is it selfish to intervene, or selfish to withhold guidance? I believe it is more loving to speak up, even when it is unwelcome.

The same applies to spouses, partners, parents, siblings, and friends. When someone we love is stuck in a self-destructive muddle, is it kinder to let them proceed at their own pace, or to use our skills to help them move forward? At times, we burn out and must step back. Perhaps true consideration lies in knowing when to intervene and when to refrain.

My 99-year-old mother recently entered a rehabilitation facility after a pelvic fracture. I pushed her to use the walker rather than rely on the wheelchair. She became furious, calling me Hitler and expressing a wish to die. Part of me wanted to withdraw and let her choose the wheelchair and diaper. But I persisted — gently, firmly — and now she is proud to be walking again and preparing to return home. It was a judgment call, informed by years of working with demoralized elderly patients. Sometimes you must push them to the brink, but not beyond.

If I were a ski, tennis, or golf professional, I would not withhold my expertise from loved ones struggling on the slopes or court. Yet when it comes to the skills of being human, pride gets in the way. Many believe they should know how to navigate life without guidance.

Labeling people as selfish or unselfish creates a false dichotomy. I see these traits on a continuum. At one extreme is pure self-interest — a life devoid of generosity, leading to alienation and guilt. At the other is complete selflessness — a martyrdom that breeds resentment. Neither extreme is sustainable.

What works is balance — the oscillation between caring for oneself and caring for others. I have lived at both ends of the continuum at times, but overall, I believe I have given much to family, friends, and patients, while also taking time to nurture myself.

Perceptions of selfishness are subjective. Children raised in the same household may view their parents differently based on their inherent neediness. Those who feel neglected may label others as selfish; those who are emotionally self-regulated rarely do.

Ultimately, whether I am selfish depends on the observer's expectations, needs, and projections. If they give from a defensive posture — trying to prove their generosity — they may see me as selfish for not matching their intensity.

From my perspective, though I have my moments, I am far from selfish. Still, it is essential to examine oneself periodically when criticism arises. Not because others are necessarily right, but because self-reflection is the cornerstone of mental health.

Addendum: Reality is shaped by language. We construct our truths through conversation and interpretation. My conclusion — that I am not selfish — is based on my criteria. Others may disagree based on their own. Searching for an ultimate truth is futile; what remains is the perspective we choose to believe. And so, the debate continues, round and round, as the world keeps turning.

THE VIRTUE OF TOLERANCE

"You have your way. I have my way. As for the right way, the correct way, and the only way — it does not exist." — Friedrich Nietzsche

The human condition, with all its quirks, imperfections, and failures, is often difficult to tolerate. We are born into a world of inevitable interpersonal discord, and none of us can escape this predicament. The quarrels, the disparities, the misunderstandings — they persist, sometimes relentlessly. Yet a fortunate minority seems to possess qualities that buffer them against the sting of intolerance. They remain calm where others react, compassionate where others condemn. What distinguishes these individuals? How do some become charitably understanding while others grow maliciously intolerant, prejudiced, or avoidant? Where does the psychodynamic structure of grudge-bearing and abusive intolerance originate?

These are not simple questions, but they are worth exploring.

We must begin with genetics. Behavioral traits often echo those of our parents and ancestors. Some temperaments are inborn, resistant to change despite the best efforts of parents, teachers, or therapists. More malleable, especially early in life, are the belief systems, cognitive values, and prejudices that shape how we interpret the world. These learned frameworks — ancestral, cultural, spiritual — determine whether we greet difference with curiosity or recoil from it in fear.

When raised in emotionally healthy environments, children learn to approach unfamiliar behavior with interest rather than dread. They develop a stable sense of worth, which reduces the need to draw others into dramatic conflict. But when children grow up in environments where expressing differences is punished or discouraged, they often become adults who cannot tolerate others' divergence. A differing point of view becomes a threat. They respond with devaluation, self-righteousness, and a compulsive need to find fault — a way to elevate themselves and quiet their own self-doubt.

Self-doubt is a powerful driver of intolerance. The zealot, the radical, the rigid ideologue — these individuals cannot endure uncertainty within themselves. They pressure others to conform to their worldview, and any resistance triggers vindictive wrath. In doing so, they reenact their own early injuries, identifying with the internalized critical parent or teacher. Now, instead of being the helpless recipient of abuse, they become the one who dishes it out. Their rigidity, hypercritical demeanor, and intolerance are predictable consequences of this history.

I often wonder what differentiates extremists from moderates within the same culture. Is there anything emotionally healthy about extremism? I suspect that most extremists are psychological misfits acting out unresolved anguish. Yet some are courageous idealists willing to risk everything to effect meaningful change. The line between a visionary and a lunatic can be thin. Even within families, an adolescent may rage or despair to shift a dysfunctional system toward health. Motives and pathology can look similar from the outside.

Consider politics. At first glance, liberals may appear more tolerant than conservatives. But in truth, liberals can be just as intolerant of conservative ideology as conservatives are of liberal principles. I have treated distressed individuals across the political spectrum. Prejudice and rigidity are not the exclusive property of any one group. They arise from personality structure, upbringing, and the need to maintain a coherent worldview — not from party affiliation.

Tolerance is not always virtuous, nor is intolerance always pathological. Accepting an abusive, self-righteous person for too long can be a sign of emotional illness. Sometimes intolerance — the refusal to endure exploitation — is the healthier choice, even if the short-term consequences are painful. I recall treating a family early in my career who finally refused to tolerate an autocratic father's abuse. Their newfound assertiveness triggered his rage, and he attempted to burn the house down. Recognizing his fragility, the family colluded to protect themselves and him. Their intolerance was necessary, but the danger was real.

Learning when to tolerate and when not to is a subtle art.

What, then, fosters tolerance? As children, if we are taught to consider another's perspective — even without certainty — we learn to interpret behavior through a compassionate lens. If we assume malicious intent, we suffer. If we assume a benign or self-protective motive, we reduce our stress and increase our capacity for understanding. Whether or not our interpretation is accurate matters less than the emotional space it creates. In the precious moments we have, why not choose the interpretation that brings peace rather than turmoil?

Some may call this naïve or self-deceptive. But when someone is truly out to harm us, refusing to play the victim often deprives them of satisfaction. They move on to someone more reactive. How we feel about another person is profoundly shaped by the intention we ascribe to their behavior.

Communication is essential. Honest, vulnerable expression fosters compassion, compromise, and forgiveness. Yet forgiveness is difficult for many. Some punish others by withholding love, friendship, or communication. They bear grudges, believing their silence will inflict meaningful suffering. But as the old saying goes, resentment is like taking poison and waiting for the other person to die. Grudge-bearing often protects against deeper pain — usually a recapitulation of childhood wounds. Healing requires addressing the original injury, not perpetuating the cycle.

As adults, we must learn that we are more durable than we once believed. The seemingly unbearable other is often just as frightened as we are, regardless of their posturing. With discipline, we can learn to observe rather than react, to tolerate rather than attack or withdraw.

Addendum: At our core, we are all children, shaped by early experiences that color our actions and reactions. These tendencies can be tamed. With awareness and effort, we can learn when tolerance is wise and when intolerance is necessary. Life is complicated. We struggle to get it right. And perhaps, before the lights go out, we finally learn to cultivate lasting, meaningful tolerance.

LIVING WITH OR WITHOUT ANOTHER — COURAGE, OR COWARD?

"For everything you have missed, you have gained something else, and for everything you gain, you lose something else." — Ralph Waldo Emerson.

Having been married, having lived in several long-term romantic relationships, and having spent a significant portion of my adult life on my own, I've come to one conclusion: it takes courage to live with another person — and perhaps even more courage to live alone.

We usually reserve the word *courage* for battle, for acts of bravery in the face of danger. But in the realm of intimate relationships, courage feels like the right word. For some, cohabitation is effortless; for others, solitude is natural and preferable. For this minority, courage is irrelevant. Living with or without another falls within a conflict-free zone, a psychological sanctuary that shields them from hazards — real or imagined — that trouble the rest of us.

God bless these lucky souls. I'm never quite sure what it takes to be so outwardly resolute. Perhaps it's genetic. Perhaps it's an uncomplicated way of viewing life. Some people accept religion without question, pray weekly, sleep soundly, and live contentedly with one partner — or alone — without a flicker of doubt about the choices they've made. It seems almost preordained, as if they slipped seamlessly into a mold shaped by parental example or early childhood security. They resist little, strive little, and accept life as it is. Zen-like. Peaceful. A remarkable gift, if authentic.

For others, the struggle is far more complex. Living with another person is no simple task. They often choose partners as complicated as themselves, stacking the deck toward intensity and effort. They would be bored without an intellectual equal — someone who challenges them, confronts them, calls them out. They thrive on nuance, drama, and the emotional texture of life. This can deepen communication, but it can also stir turmoil. The sword cuts both ways.

On the other side of courage lies cowardice — a word that can apply equally to living with someone or living alone. The fear of dealing with another's complexities — control, responsibility, sensitivity, criticism, rejection, abandonment — can be overwhelming. Childhood traumas often shape adults who are overly sensitive to these dynamics, making cohabitation feel perilous. For them, avoidance becomes a form of self-protection, a retreat from the emotional demands of intimacy.

Learning to compromise, communicate clearly, and navigate conflict is painful. For some, the process becomes so excruciating that they develop a phobic avoidance of cohabitation. From the outside, this may look like cowardice. But appearances deceive.

Consider the young adult who moves directly from the parental home into a relationship. Some would call that cowardice — an unwillingness to face life alone. Yet spending time in solitude, confronting loneliness, and taking full responsibility for one's life can be profoundly character-building. What initially appears cowardly may ultimately be courageous.

It depends on how you look at it.

What seems courageous to one person may appear spineless to another. We cannot force someone to be braver than their psychological ecology allows. The human condition is fragile. Pushing someone beyond their limits can trigger emotional collapse, despair, or physical stress reactions. Respecting another's capacity — or lack thereof — is essential.

Our approach to life works for us, but not necessarily for others. Some people lack the skills to sustain long-term relationships; others cannot bear solitude. Life's twists and turns may eventually teach them new ways of living, but until then, we can encourage without pushing, support without coercing.

Courage and cowardice do not arise in a vacuum. They evolve from a lifetime of genetic, biochemical, environmental, and social influences. We are all fragile souls, struggling to navigate the harsh realities of existence. These states — courage and cowardice — are fluid, not fixed. A person terrified of living alone may eventually find the courage to do so. Someone afraid of intimacy may one day risk a partnership. Pain often catalyzes transformation.

Living alone too long can spark a yearning for companionship. Living with another person for too long can ignite a longing for solitude. Cowardice morphs into courage, and courage into cowardice, depending on the moment and the need.

Addendum: Both living alone and living with another are battles of their own. In truth, we are all cowards and all courageous at different times. What matters is recognizing how difficult life can be — how often we recoil in fear, and how often we push forward despite it. If we are fortunate, we reach the end able to say, without equivocation, that the struggle was worth it. Slaying the dragon — whatever form it takes — allows us to feel, if only briefly, like courageous heroes rather than failed cowards.

A TIME TO RESIST, A TIME TO ACCEPT

"Do not go gentle into that good night. Rage, rage against the dying of the light."
— Dylan Thomas

Life, for most of us, is an ever-present struggle — a landscape of twists and turns that rarely unfolds the way we imagined. Repeatedly, we find ourselves confronting circumstances far beyond our control. And in those moments, we tend to fall into one of two camps: those who resist with every fiber of their being, and those who surrender to what is.

Some of us fight tooth and nail, rejecting the circumstances that have fallen upon us, determined to undo or minimize the gravity of the situation. Others relinquish the need for control, placing their fate in the hands of God, destiny, or "the universe," trusting that acceptance will bring peace where resistance cannot.

From the outside, acceptance may look like resignation. From the inside, it may feel like serenity. Those inclined to accept often view the fighters as clinging to the illusion that they can do more than is humanly possible. The fighters, in turn, see the acceptors as prematurely defeated — passive, depressed, or lacking the vigor to push toward a constructive outcome.

Perhaps both responses are simply variations of the ancient fight-or-flight reflex, shaped by temperament, biology, upbringing, and the psychological scaffolding laid down in childhood.

What motivated me to write this essay — then and now — is the desire to understand the difference between these two orientations. What determines whether we resist or accept? What are the costs and benefits of each? And beneath that intellectual inquiry lies something more personal: a familiar self-interrogation triggered by witnessing someone else's way of coping. Their style stirs a question in me — a dollop of doubt — about my own modus operandi and what I might learn from it.

From the very beginning of life, temperament asserts itself. Some infants — even in utero — are more active, more restless, more determined. Others are quieter, more yielding. These tendencies often persist into adulthood. The active individual exhausts every option before surrendering. If they finally give in, it is only because their body or time has run out. The more passive individual abdicates control earlier, placing their fate in divine hands. If life is predetermined, they reason, then acceptance is wisdom.

Prayer, faith, and surrender are not to be disparaged — unless they prevent us from pursuing options that might truly make a difference. Solace is something we all need to navigate life's complexities.

"Praise the Lord and pass the ammunition," the saying goes. I have always subscribed to that duality. I will ask for help from whatever invisible force governs the universe, but I will also fight with everything I have. That stance was forged early. Raised by a loving mother who could not fully protect me, I learned to survive on my own. I developed fierce independence, a drive to slay dragons before they slayed me. Denial was not a luxury I possessed. I had to beat reality before it beat me.

It was stressful — and I suspect it left its mark on my protoplasm, contributing to the degenerative disc disease and other bodily aberrations that arrived later. Even death offered no refuge. As a child, I lay awake at night, terrified of ceasing to exist, envious of those who claimed not to think about it at all. Did they possess a security I lacked? A capacity for denial that eluded me.

Those who believe in an afterlife, reincarnation, or a resting place for the soul often accept fate more easily. I envied them. I could never buy into those beliefs, no matter how much I wanted to. Their certainty felt smug, even arrogant, as if they knew something I did not. How could they be so sure? How could they glide so gently into the night while I raged against the dying of the light?

Fighting the uncontrollable forces of life can be exhausting — and often futile. In athletics, in medicine, in every arena where I pushed myself, I fought to be the best I could be. When I fell short, humiliation and self-flagellation were never far behind. Accepting limitations — without believing I was better than the way I was showing up — was never easy.

When you spend a lifetime mastering challenges through effort and will, it is difficult to accept the ravages of age, the betrayals of the body, or even the maddening game of golf. Learning to observe one's limitations without harsh judgment is a worthy goal, even if it runs counter to a lifelong combatant stance.

It has been said that you don't truly have something until you can let it go. I have held on to achievement so tightly that, at times, it has slipped through my fingers. I am learning — slowly — to hold things more lightly, to allow calm acceptance to temper the relentless drive that once served me but now threatens to burn me out.

It is, as always, a matter of balance. We must fight hard when fighting is necessary, and we must know when to step back and accept what is. Too much fight is as dangerous as too much flight. Premature acceptance can prevent us from unraveling a solvable problem; relentless resistance can destroy us.

The single-minded warrior must be tempered by the calm witness. After the storm of effort, acceptance creates a respite — a place to regroup before choosing the next step.

Yes, we can rage against the dying of the light. But eventually, we must allow ourselves to go gently into the night. The night is inevitable for all of us, often heralded by the slow slither of decrepitude that eclipses our former vigor. We grieve that loss. But for the time that remains, we must accept where we are, acknowledge it deeply, and find peace in the remarkable, difficult journey we have traveled.

Addendum: On the heels of writing this essay, I wonder how much easier life would be if I simply coasted — if I didn't ponder these imponderables, ask these questions, or wrestle with these contradictions. How many people spend as much time as I do trying to comprehend these tensions? Perhaps many. Perhaps few. But in the end, it makes no difference. If writing brings clarity, satisfaction, or even a moment of peace, then something meaningful has come from the struggle.

REACTIVE REMEDIATION

"A life of reaction is a life of slavery, intellectually and spiritually. One must fight for a life of action, not reaction." — Rita Mae Brown.

We are all so deeply human that we inevitably fall prey to emotional reactivity — those impulsive responses that far exceed the stimulus at hand. In childhood and adolescence, this vulnerability is expected. Young people deflect feelings of smallness and inadequacy with thin-skinned reactivity, a natural byproduct of egocentric development. Ideally, this diminishes with maturity as we learn to separate our internal world from others' entanglements.

But for some, that sticky enmeshment lingers. It can persist into adolescence and adulthood, and sometimes never dissipates at all. When reactivity becomes woven into the fabric of one's character, extinguishing it becomes a formidable challenge.

The first truth we must acknowledge is that reactivity rarely accomplishes anything beyond alienating others. Yet if alienation has been our lifelong pattern, giving it up can feel like a threat to our very identity. It is tragic how easily one can become addicted to self-destructive modes of operating. The longer they persist, the harder it is to relinquish. Without viable, repeatable alternatives, the odds of regression and relapse remain high.

Many factors contribute to emotional reactivity. Some inherit a nervous system exquisitely sensitive to stimuli, deprivation, or assault. Early parental care — or the lack of it — shapes our most vulnerable years. Excessive frustration, neglect, or aggression can leave a child emotionally raw, predisposed to overreactivity. Later traumas — war, loss, illness, upheaval — further erode tolerance, leaving the adult thin-skinned and easily overwhelmed.

Whatever the origins, the goal is the same: to interrupt the pattern and diminish, if not eliminate, this destructive predisposition. But not everyone is amenable to change. Individuals with longstanding personality disorders or biochemical vulnerabilities often struggle to regulate their moods. They live at the mercy of their reactive hurt and anger, their defensive postures shielding a core of inadequacy, loneliness, and fear of rejection.

Like all psychological traits, narcissistic defenses exist on a continuum. Some are mild and responsive to intervention; others are severe, requiring years of intensive therapy — sometimes with limited success.

For healthier, higher-functioning individuals, change is possible. They can learn stop-gap strategies that allow them to pause, reflect, and choose a response rather than react impulsively. These individuals possess enough psychological insight to recognize the destructiveness of their patterns. They may initially blame the other person — the stimulus — but eventually retract the projection, take ownership of their part, and take steps toward healthier behavior.

What are those steps?

First, one must become conscious of the egocentric nature of overreactivity. Overreactors are trapped in dramatic internal scripts, preoccupied with personalized narratives that distort their perception of events. Their assumptions prevent them from exploring what has transpired.

The antidote begins with silence. When the emotional storm has passed, clear your mind of assumptions, look at the other person, and ask softly and sincerely:

- "What's going on?"
- "What am I failing to give you that you need?"
- "Help me understand."
- "What can I do to make you happy?

The overreactive person can ask themselves:

- "What do I want that I'm not getting?"
- "What do I need to feel content in this moment?"

These questions shift the focus from self-oriented reactivity to curiosity and consideration. They transform aggression into inquiry. And if the reaction has already occurred, one can still salvage the moment by asking aloud:

- "Why am I reacting this way? What do I want that I'm not getting?"

In my experience, the other person is often relieved — even grateful — when we show a willingness to examine ourselves. A heartfelt apology, grounded in genuine curiosity, can be profoundly healing. Frustration, anger, anxiety, and depression often stem from unmet needs or the fear of future deprivation. The only path to resolution is open dialogue.

One of the most transformative exercises I used with couples was this:

"Pretend you can get whatever you want from your partner, and all you have to do is change one thing about yourself. What would that be?"

This reframes the dynamic entirely. Instead of trying to change the other, each person focuses on altering themselves. Remarkably, their answers often align with what the partner had silently wished for all along.

Most of us know exactly what we need to do to make our partner happy. Yet we withhold it. Why? Because giving it feels risky. It may expose shame, vulnerability, or fear. One patient once told his wife, "If I open up and reveal my feelings, I'll lose my autonomy. I'll feel like a child again." His withholding was rooted in fear, not malice.

When one partner is predisposed to abandonment fears and the other to emotional withholding, the result is predictable: frustration, pain, and overreactivity. These patterns are often complementary — two sides of the same coin, both rooted in childhood narcissistic injury. Healing requires both individuals to confront their sensitivities and defenses.

For some, the damage is too serious. The familiar misery of reenacting childhood scripts may feel safer than the unknown territory of healthier relating.

But for many, remediation is possible — provided the underlying pathology is not so severe as to require long-term reconstructive psychotherapy. And even then, we lose nothing by trying.

Addendum: It takes patience and willingness to stay present when an emotional flare-up hijacks a conversation. Using these skills is benevolent but time-consuming. I am willing to do it for those who matter most in my life, but no longer for everyone, as I did in my psychiatric practice. Some challenges are gratifying; others are draining. As we age, relaxation often trumps the adrenaline rush of conflict. Too much challenge is stressful; too much ease is dull. Once again, life demands balance — the lifelong, delicate balancing act.

CURIOSITY AND ITS DETERMINANTS — ASSET OR LIABILITY?

"I keep six honest serving men, They taught me all I knew. Their names are What, Why, and When and How and Where and Who." — Rudyard Kipling.

Curiosity — the desire to know, to understand, to inquire — is one of the most intriguing aspects of the human condition. What first drew me to examine curiosity itself was observing how differently people relate to one another along the spectrum of being *interested* versus being *interesting*. Some individuals seem naturally inquisitive, eager to understand the person before them. Others appear utterly uninterested, absorbed in their own narrative, indifferent to the inner world of the person they're speaking with.

What accounts for this disparity?

Perhaps some were raised by parents so fascinated with them that they never learned to look outward. If a child grows up believing the world is as captivated by their minutiae as their parents were, they may develop poor listening skills and an inflated sense of self-importance. Conversely, a child raised in a household that devalues individual expression — *Why would anyone care about what you think?* You may grow into an adult who speaks only about others, rarely revealing anything personal.

Some families go further still: *Be seen and not heard. Stop prying. Don't be nosy. Curiosity killed the cat.* These injunctions stifle inquisitiveness early on. To avoid being probed by others, such individuals may fill every silence with talk, taking up all the air in the room.

Culture also shapes curiosity. What is discussable today — sex, dysfunction, bodily ailments — would have been taboo fifty years ago. A liberal culture encourages inquiry; a conservative one may suppress it. Under the guise of privacy, some become secretive, assuming others are equally guarded, and thus never ask.

I believe the curious mind emerges early. Some children ask endless questions; others quietly gather information on their own. Even within the same family, curiosity varies. During medical school, I noticed how some students asked questions freely, unconcerned about appearing foolish, while others remained silent, preferring confusion to vulnerability. I admired the former. Their curiosity accelerated their learning.

What inspired this essay was observing individuals who crave attention yet show little interest in reciprocating. I wondered whether this was a narcissistic trait — a fixed personality style — or a temporary state. After seeing the same pattern across contexts, I concluded that for many, it is not easily reprogrammable. When I gently pointed it out, some appreciated the feedback; others reacted with bewilderment or wounded pride.

Sometimes curiosity is blocked by the assumption that one already knows who the other person is — a grandiose belief devoid of reality testing. Many form conclusions without ever checking them out conversationally, creating unnecessary interpersonal havoc. Others, driven by insecurity, are hypercurious about what others think of them, a pattern that can range from neurotic self-esteem issues to paranoid ideation.

At times, I wish I could view all human behavior — narcissistic or otherwise — as pure artistic expression, the full spectrum of humanity painted across a vast canvas. Andy Warhol seemed to possess that capacity: to appreciate all forms of expression, however odd or unattractive, as manifestations of a divine creative soul. How spiritual, how forgiving, how free of preconceived notions. I doubt I will ever reach that level of equanimity. I have my preferences, and I gravitate toward those who show genuine interest in others.

Self-interest is essential; it provides confidence and vitality. But without an equal interest in others, one risks becoming truly self-centered. Self-centered people can be fascinating — for a while. They spin captivating stories, but without moments of mutuality, their charm fades. Eventually, they must seek a new audience, as the old one tires and moves on.

So, is curiosity an asset or a liability?

It depends on calibration. Children ask questions without judgment; adults must learn when curiosity is welcome and when it intrudes. When curiosity is appreciated, it is undeniably an asset. When it provokes admonitions — *Don't pry, mind your business* — it can feel like a liability. But even then, for those who view curiosity as a path to growth, it remains a gift.

From my perspective, being genuinely interested in others is a profound asset. The absence of that desire is a liability — though I admit my bias as a psychiatrist whose profession rests on curiosity and a burning desire to understand the human condition.

Perhaps the lesson for me is to remain curious not only about others, but about why some people show so little curiosity themselves. Maintaining the observer role — as I did for forty years — protects the psyche. The downside is that it can keep others at a distance, limiting the possibility of an authentic, intimate connection.

Knowing whom to keep at bay and whom to open up to is a crucial judgment call. Sometimes we misjudge and enter dysfunctional interactions. Attempts at honest communication may backfire, prompting us to minimize contact when we realize that healthy relating is unlikely.

Addendum: As with all my essays, I write without an outline, not knowing where the piece will end. Each essay helps me work through an issue, so it doesn't linger unresolved, gnawing at my psyche. After writing, reviewing, and digesting what emerges, I feel lighter — not unlike the relief I once felt after a good session with my psychoanalyst.

CRITERIA AND BEYOND IN THE PURSUIT OF A RELATIONSHIP

"Man is unique in that he has plans, purpose, and goals that require the need for criteria of choice. The need for ethical value is within man whose future may largely be determined by the choice he makes." — George Bernard Shaw.

Choosing a relationship — whether in love, work, or friendship — is a complex psychological process shaped by a constellation of criteria. Consciously, we believe we know what we're looking for. We set benchmarks, mental checklists, and standards that help us decide whether someone meets the threshold for connection. But beneath the surface, unconscious forces, past experiences, and deeply embedded expectations shape our choices just as powerfully.

Some people can size up a situation instantly. They know what they want and what they will not tolerate. Others need time — sometimes a great deal of it — to discern whether a relationship fits. Criteria can be constructive or destructive, depending on the health of the individual and the experiences that built their internal "criteria bank."

The longer one lives, the more complex that bank becomes. A person who has tasted the finest food and wine becomes more discerning than someone with limited exposure. A trained musician hears subtleties others miss. A dancer sees nuance invisible to the untrained eye. And someone who has been in many relationships — long and short, passionate and quiet, joyful and painful — carries a vast internal archive of comparisons.

This essay explores how one chooses a woman after having known so many, each leaving behind a residue of sensory, emotional, and intellectual impressions that inevitably shape the evaluation of anyone new.

Over the years, I have known women who were brilliant thinkers, gifted communicators, extraordinary lovers, nurturing souls, loyal companions, and best friends in every sense. Some were athletes with boundless energy; others danced with such grace that I felt, for fleeting moments, like Fred to their Ginger. One was a culinary magician; another offered touch, comfort, and warmth with effortless generosity. Some were breathtakingly beautiful. Each had something exceptional — though none had everything.

And who am I to expect "everything" in one person? I, too, am imperfect. I fall short of my own criteria. I can be reactive, intolerant of quirks that don't match my past experiences, and quick to exit when a relationship diverges from the narrative I've constructed about the mythical woman with the golden apples — the one who meets every criterion par excellence.

Certain criteria, however, are non-negotiable: keeping one's word, reliability, faithfulness, and integrity. When these are missing, friendships falter.

Now older, softened and scarred by time, I tell myself I should be grateful for a good woman who loves and appreciates me. But gratitude does not come easily when the remnants of a younger, more confident self still whisper that settling is a betrayal. Voltaire's warning — *the perfect is the enemy of the good* — has not fully taken root.

I sometimes marvel at people who find a partner quickly, settle in, and never look back. How do they do that? Perhaps humility plays a role — gratitude for being loved, acceptance of human imperfection, a capacity to live with another's idiosyncrasies. The clock is ticking; change must come sooner rather than later if companionship is to be part of the final chapters.

I spend a great deal of time examining what I want. Perhaps I should spend more time examining what I do *not* want — the criteria that quietly sabotage my willingness to commit.

Freedom is one such criterion. Living alone offers delicious autonomy: doing what I want, when I want, without negotiation. For someone like me, this freedom can interfere with cohabitation.

Another factor is how one tolerates solitude. For some, living alone is painful and accelerates the desire to bond. For others — me included — solitude can be deeply satisfying. The need for companionship is less urgent.

Social context also plays a role. In certain communities, being single or dating multiple women is frowned upon; in more cosmopolitan circles, individuality is celebrated. Feeling comfortable as the "odd man out" reduces the pressure to pair up. Being at ease going solo — socially and emotionally — diminishes the sense of urgency.

Familiarity is another determinant. As an only child, I learned early to entertain myself, to find comfort in solitude. That comfort can become a preferred state. Conversely, those from large families often recreate the bustle of their upbringing through marriage and children. Neuroplasticity allows us to adapt to new arrangements, but only if introduced gradually, without shocking the system.

Growing up in a divorced home adds another layer. Without a model for long-term cohesion, one may internalize a script that normalizes separation. Add to that the antiquated court system — designed to protect children but often punishing men financially — and the incentive to avoid remarriage becomes stronger. Cynicism replaces romantic idealism.

This entire exercise — examining criteria, dissecting preferences, analyzing past and present — may be a red herring. A wild-goose chase. Perhaps I am simply one point on the vast spectrum of human relational patterns. Some couples do; some do not. Some settle early, others late, others never. The rest is speculation.

And then there is the perennial question of free will. Do we truly choose? Or are our decisions reactive products of accumulated experience, unconscious forces, and chance?

Addendum: When perplexed, I think my way through the problem. Eventually, I convince myself I understand why things unfolded as they did — though who really knows? Life seems to be a blend of choice, chance, and unconscious determinants. We show up where we show up. It might be easier to simply accept things as they are and see what comes next, rather than believing that analysis will alter the future. Maybe it will; maybe it won't. But for me, the mental exercise is pleasurable — a way to keep my mind active in retirement, just as golf and the gym keep my body moving. I think, I feel, I write — and if nothing else, no harm is done.

OUR NARRATIVE — HONEST OR NOT?

"When one door of happiness closes, another opens, but often we look so long at the closed door that we do not see the one that has been opened for us." — Helen Keller.

Perhaps it is a lifelong quandary, or perhaps it becomes more pronounced as we age. Lately, I've become increasingly aware of the dissonance between who we are and who we have been. We often feel tethered to our past selves, nostalgically connected to earlier versions of our identity. As a result, we continue to believe we are, in many ways, the embodiment of who we once were.

Are we entitled to hold on to the identity of our vigorous youth — the athletic, energetic, sexually potent self — even as age inevitably erodes those capacities? Or must we, with honesty and humility, relinquish that earlier image and accept that it no longer represents our current reality?

A parallel absurdity also exists: we sometimes believe we have already become the person we aspire to be, when in truth, we are not nearly as far along as we imagine. We rush toward new goals, striving for fresh accomplishments, while simultaneously clinging to the glory of our past. We want to be both who we were and who we hope to become, without acknowledging the gap between the two.

Each of us carries a conscious and unconscious narrative about who we are. We hold memories — some accurate, some embellished — of who we once were. We harbor fantasies of who we want to become. And we make ongoing attempts to recognize who we truly are in the present. Most of us maintain a blend of truth and distortion, a narrative that is part autobiography, part fiction.

Recently, I rewatched the 2003 film *Something's Gotta Give*. In one scene, Harry — Jack Nicholson's aging Lothario — lands in the emergency room with an anxiety attack. A young nurse tells him, "If you were my dad, I'd send you home to recuperate." Harry, stunned, repeats, "If I were your dad?" The implication clashes violently with the narrative he has constructed about himself: the eternally virile man who dates women half his age. Only when confronted with his mortality does he allow himself to pursue Erica, a woman closer to his own age. Life forces his narrative to shift.

In many ways, my life mirrored Harry's. I, too, have avoided committing to age-appropriate women, clinging to the storyline I created about myself. I still see myself as young and vital, though the truth is more complicated. I am no longer the man who ran marathons, telemark-skied double diamonds, or made love all night. The memories feel recent, but the years — and the injuries — tell another story. I remain identified with that athletic, virile man, reluctant to let go of the image. Qualitatively, I may still feel like him; quantitatively, I am not.

Another form of narrative distortion occurs when we prematurely believe we have achieved our aspirations. A few good rounds of golf, and we imagine we've arrived — only to be humbled the following week. Self-deception is a convenient tool for bolstering self-esteem, especially when it falters. It ranges from mild exaggeration to full-blown delusion.

The other day, I spoke with a beautiful young Swiss yoga instructor. When she told me she could ski before she could walk, she asked if I skied. I immediately replied, "Yes, for many years. Telemark since 1977." She was impressed. I felt a surge of exhilaration, as if I were back in the game. If she invited me to ski with her, I would likely push myself recklessly, trying to match her down the mountain, risking catastrophic injury to preserve the illusion of who I once was. The male ego is astonishingly foolish. Men have literally died trying to impress younger women — a final, misguided attempt to resurrect youth.

I didn't tell her that I now ski infrequently, or that my knee, back, and cervical spine are far more fragile than they once were. The wiser adaptation would be to bow out of such temptations, acknowledging the vulnerability that comes with age.

Recently, at the gym, I spoke with another retired physician. We both still maintain our medical licenses, despite knowing we will likely never practice again. Being a physician is so deeply woven into our identity that letting go of the license feels like another small death. I still feel like a psychiatrist, though it has been years since I treated a patient. Will I return to practice? Perhaps. Or perhaps that is another self-deception. The boundary between who we were, who we are, and who we will be becomes increasingly blurry.

Letting go is rarely swift. It is a slow, reluctant process, filled with resistance. Yet without letting go, we risk living inside a narrative that no longer fits.

Addendum: With so much in life, we straddle the line between resistance and acceptance. The longer we resist, the more we suffer; the sooner we accept, the more peace we find. Can we accelerate this process? I'm not sure. Perhaps the speed of resolution is determined by our inborn characterological coping style — the way we metabolize stress, loss, and change. And since character rarely changes, perhaps the only answer is patience: patience with ourselves as we face the truth of who we were, who we are, and who we are becoming.

NOW WHAT

"Everything flows, and nothing abides; everything gives way, and nothing stays fixed." — Heraclitus (c. 540–c 475 BC)

We strive, we climb, we accomplish. We reach the top of the mountain — sometimes literally, sometimes metaphorically — and expect elation, fulfillment, a sense of having finally arrived. Yet the thrill is often brief, far shorter than we imagined. The summit, once reached, rarely delivers the sustained ecstasy we anticipated.

Peggy Lee captured this disillusionment in her 1969 song: *"Is that all there is? If that's all there is, my friend, then let's keep dancing."* When I first heard it, I was too young to understand. Now, decades later, it resonates with unnerving clarity. The song speaks to the universal disappointment that follows experiences we once believed would be singular, transformative, or permanently gratifying.

As children, we dream of love, family, success, power, prestige, joy — the full banquet of life's offerings. When we lack these things, we imagine that acquiring them will be the key to happiness. And when we finally do acquire them — the travel, the adventures, the sensual pleasures, the luxuries — the exhilaration is real, but fleeting.

Skiing in Aspen and Vail. Boating, hiking, and biking across continents. Exquisite meals seasoned with spices from every corner of the world. Custom-tailored clothing. Beautiful women. Sexual delights. A Porsche, a Mercedes. Cuban cigars, fine cognac, and a bottle of Château d'Yquem on a special night. Oceanfront living. Trips to New York, London, Paris — museums, music, theater, restaurants. Golf, polo, and equestrian events. Rubbing shoulders with the rich and famous.

Now what?

Kirk Douglas once said he enjoyed the fantasy of accomplishment more than the accomplishment itself. I understand that now. The marriage, the family, the material acquisitions, the prestige, the hole-in-one — they are all illusions of permanence, short-term highs that fade. *Is that all there is?*

Yes — and no.

Yes, in the sense that no experience, no matter how extraordinary, can sustain its initial intensity. Impermanence is the rule. Everything flows; nothing abides. Life gives us a taste of ecstasy, then snatches it away. The only thing that endures is the present moment — and even that slips through our fingers the instant we lose awareness.

The process of striving is the body of life; the outcome is merely punctuation. Children grow up and leave; we enjoy them, then let them go. If they return, we savor it, then release it again. Relationships flourish or falter, revive or die. Loved ones passed. Fortunes rise and fall. Even the most breathtaking views — ocean horizons, snowcapped mountains — eventually become background scenery. Nothing sustains the childlike *wow* for long.

So, we seek new heights: new tastes, new textures, new experiences. The unfamiliar becomes the preferred terrain of the jaded. A friend once took me to Chinatown in Flushing, Queens, where I tasted beef tendons in hot chili oil — an unfamiliar texture, a revelation. Novelty becomes its own addiction.

There's a story of a man who works his entire life to retire to a Caribbean island, eat, drink, relax, enjoy his family, and go fishing. When he shares this dream with a local fisherman, the old man replies, "Sir, I've been doing that my entire life. I just never had to work so hard to get here."

As a boy, I had few material possessions, yet I laughed, played, and felt content. I envied my wealthier friends — their boats, their clubs, their fancy homes. Now that I've lived that life, I wonder how much better off they truly were. Privilege from birth may be easier to attain than later, but the end result is the same: impermanence.

Would I have preferred the silver spoon? Perhaps. It might have made me a better golfer, spared me years of struggle. But even if I became a great golfer now, how long would the satisfaction last? A week? A month? Accomplishments fade like everything else.

And so, we return to Sisyphus. Camus imagined him happy — not because the boulder stays at the top, but because the struggle itself fills his heart. The climb gives life meaning, not the summit.

Fresh challenges will come. They will offer their brief exhilaration. And then the question will return: *Is that all there is?* The answer, inevitably, is yes — because the only permanent truth is change.

Addendum: After writing this essay, I felt unsettled by its cynicism. It seemed like a cul-de-sac — a dead end with no hope of more. But perhaps there is more. Perhaps the "more" lies not in novelty or acquisition, but in depth, presence, connection, and meaning. I need to write further, to re-examine this conclusion. The inquiry continues.

REMEDIAL GRATITUDE

"If the only prayer you said in your whole life was, Thank you, that would suffice." — Meister Eckhart.

After writing my previous essay, *Now What?* I found myself wondering how to keep that disillusioned refrain — *"Is that all there is?"* — from echoing in the background. If impermanence is the rule, if the thrill of life's pleasures inevitably fades, is it possible to sustain delight without watching it dissolve into ennui?

A sunset, a perfect day, a wonderful meal, a meaningful conversation — all can lose their sparkle when repeated often enough. We begin to take them for granted, forgetting that each one is a gift, not a guarantee.

Life, with its twists and turns, eventually brings us to the threshold of appreciation. Time runs down. Loved ones die. Loss becomes a teacher. I no longer take a round of golf for granted, nor do I complain as much about a bad bounce or a lousy shot. Instead, I find myself thinking how lucky I am to be here, still able to play. Barry — a dear friend and longtime golf companion — is gone now. In his absence, he left me with a legacy of gratitude.

Other memories of friends and relatives who died young have had a similar effect. Their absence sharpens my appreciation for the ability to do what they once loved. Sometimes I even find myself doing things I normally wouldn't, simply to feel reconnected to them.

The other night, I bought Hebrew National franks, Heinz beans, potato salad, and sauerkraut — one of my mother's favorite meals. Far too much salt and nitrite for any sensible diet, yet she lived to 101. I devoured it with gusto, and for a moment, it felt as if she were sitting beside me. A simple meal, never to be replicated in quite the same way, became a portal to memory — and a reminder that I am still here to enjoy it.

I think of friends who died before they could watch their children grow. I look at my daughter now with a renewed sense of gratitude, shaped by the awareness that others never had this privilege.

With age comes the inevitability of medical issues and the proximity of death. These realities teach us to be thankful. Gratitude becomes a lens that alters perception, allowing us to savor life moment by moment. From that vantage point, everything we do is a gift — as long as we are still breathing.

Whether one attributes this to luck, chance, or divine blessing, the conclusion is the same: we are fortunate. The more I reflect on Peggy Lee's *"Is That All There Is?"*, the more I see the sadness in that jaded resignation. Yet perhaps that disillusionment is a necessary prelude to a deeper, more mature appreciation — a shift from novelty-seeking to gratitude.

My earlier conclusion — that after achieving much of what I wanted, all that remained was disillusionment — now feels incomplete. Everything is impermanent. Everything changes. Nothing stays fixed. We cling to people, objects, and identities in an attempt to deny frailty and death, only to be disappointed when they slip away.

Jean-Baptiste Alphonse Karr wrote, *"The more things change, the more they stay the same."* But the one thing that never changes is change itself. Since we are different from day to day, our perception of reality is always in flux. And because we are always changing, the same experience can feel new again — if we meet it with gratitude.

This, I believe, is the "more" that follows *"Is that all there is?"* Not more possessions, more thrills, more novelty — but more depth. More presence. More appreciation. More awareness that we are never the same person twice.

A full supermoon over the Miami ocean — something I've seen countless times — becomes awe-inspiring again when viewed through gratitude. *Thank you* becomes a prayer, a mantra, a way of seeing.

Thank you for another day. Thank you for breath. Thank you for the chance to witness beauty that so many sick or dying people would give anything to experience.

With the awe of a child, we grow older, wiser, and recapture our *wow*.

Addendum: A Zen parable tells of a man chased by a tiger. He grabs a vine over a cliff, only to find another tiger waiting below. Two mice — one white, one black — begin gnawing at the vine. In that precarious moment, he notices a ripe strawberry. Holding the vine with one hand, he plucks the strawberry with the other, tastes it, and says, *"My God, how sweet it is."* That is gratitude — not denial of danger, but the ability to savor sweetness even as the vine frays.

STUFF AND SEARCH FOR SIMPLICITY

"Have nothing in your houses that you do not know to be useful or believe to be beautiful." — William Morris

I have spent a lifetime accumulating things — objects that once felt essential, symbolic, comforting, or simply pleasurable. Books, art, clothing, furniture, gadgets, mementos, collections of every kind. Each item carried a story, a memory, a justification. And for years, I believed these possessions enriched my life.

But lately, I've begun to question that assumption.

There comes a point — often in later life, sometimes earlier — when the sheer volume of accumulated "stuff" becomes burdensome. Not just physically, but psychologically. Closets, drawers, cabinets, and storage units begin to feel like extensions of the mind: cluttered, overfilled, weighed down by the sediment of decades.

I once thought of myself as a curator of my own life — someone who surrounded himself with objects that reflected taste, history, and identity. But now I see that much of what I kept was less about appreciation and more about attachment. A fear of letting go. A belief that discarding an object meant discarding the memory attached to it.

It doesn't.

If anything, the opposite is true. The fewer objects I keep, the more clearly I remember the ones that matter.

Some possessions still bring joy: a piece of art that stirs emotion, a well-worn sweater that carries the scent of winter, a book whose margins hold the handwriting of my younger self. But many items — perhaps most — have outlived their purpose. They sit untouched, unneeded, unmissed.

Why, then, do we hold on?

Part of it is habit. Part is sentimentality. Part is the illusion is that our possessions protect us from the passage of time. And part is the quiet fear that without our things, we might feel exposed — stripped of the identity we spent years constructing.

But simplicity has its own seduction.

There is a lightness that comes from letting go, a clarity that emerges when the unnecessary falls away. I've begun to feel it in small ways: clearing a drawer, donating clothes, giving away books I once believed I'd reread. Each act of release creates a little more space — not just in the home, but in the psyche.

I've also noticed something else: the more I let go, the more I appreciate what remains.

A single object, chosen with intention, carries more meaning than a dozen chosen out of habit. A room with space to breathe feels more peaceful than one filled with relics of former selves. And a life with fewer possessions feels — paradoxically — more abundant.

This shift is not about asceticism. It's about discernment. It's about recognizing that the pursuit of simplicity is, at its core, a pursuit of freedom.

Freedom from clutter. Freedom from obligation. Freedom from the weight of the past. Freedom to move, to adapt, to live with greater ease.

I sometimes wonder what my daughter will think when she eventually sorts through my belongings. Will she feel burdened? Overwhelmed? Saddled with the task of deciphering what mattered to me and what didn't. The thought alone is enough to motivate further pruning.

Simplicity is not just a personal preference; it is an act of kindness toward those who will one day inherit the remnants of our lives.

I am not yet where I want to be. I still cling to more than I need. But I am learning — slowly, deliberately — to let go. To keep only what is useful, beautiful, or deeply meaningful. To release the rest with gratitude for the role it once played.

Addendum: The search for simplicity is ongoing. It is less about achieving a perfect state of minimalism and more about cultivating awareness — noticing what we carry, why we carry it, and how it shapes the way we live. Each discarded object is a small liberation. Each act of letting go is a quiet step toward a lighter, more intentional life.

BEING A PSYCHIATRIST

"A psychiatrist is a man who goes to the Folies Bergère and looks at the audience." — Mervyn Stockwood.

There is, in my view, a very fine line between being a psychiatrist and being a patient. It is a line we must never lose sight of, lest we fall into the trap of imagining ourselves superior to the people who have entrusted us with their most private inner worlds. Too often, to my dismay, I heard colleagues refer to their patients as "crazies," as if the dividing line were thick and impenetrable. In truth, it is thin. But for the grace of genetics, biochemistry, childhood circumstance, and sheer luck, any one of us could have ended up on the other side of the couch.

My desire to become a psychiatrist was driven by multiple factors. On the surface, I admired the noble portrayal of psychiatrists in the films of the 1950s — dignified, wise, untainted by the cynicism that later eras would attach to the profession. But beneath that veneer lay something more personal. My mother always seemed to have an answer for everything related to human behavior, and I found myself determined to understand the human condition better than she did. Perhaps I wanted to prove her wrong. Perhaps I wanted to understand why she believed she was always right. To this day, I bristle at anyone who claims to have the answers to life's most difficult questions.

Growing up in a household where conversations often revolved around why people behaved as they did, I naturally became curious. Psychiatry became the logical extension of that early fascination. I would like to say my motives were purely altruistic, but honesty compels me to admit that neurotic curiosity played a significant role.

In medical school, I flirted with Neurology and Internal Medicine — specialties that appealed to my cerebral inclinations — but ultimately accepted a psychiatry residency. Columbia Presbyterian offered me a position at the adjacent Neurological Institute, and I came close to switching. The neurologists seemed more grounded, less spooky, less entangled in their own psychological webs. But I stayed the course.

Psychiatric residency was its own universe. The old joke — one psychiatrist says, "Good morning," and the other replies, "I wonder what he meant by that" — captured the atmosphere perfectly. Everyone was analyzing everyone else. Some professors thrived on intimidation, projecting their unresolved demons onto vulnerable residents. One particularly daunting professor turned out to be the milder version of his own father. We were simply the recipients of his inherited torment.

Psychoanalysis was at its peak in the early 1960s, and undergoing personal analysis was considered a moral imperative. For seven years, five days a week, I lay on the couch staring at the ceiling, saying whatever came to mind. My analyst — a traditional Washington Psychoanalytic Institute figure — spoke sparingly, serving as a blank screen for my projections. His silence was maddening. For months, I tried to get him to speak. When I finally surrendered and said, "There is absolutely nothing I can do to make you talk," he replied, "Oh, you've noticed?" A costly but invaluable lesson in relinquishing control.

My analysis continued through my selective service stint at the National Institute of Mental Health and into my private practice in Washington, D.C. The practice grew quickly; soon, I had a waiting list. I felt honored that so many trusted me with their inner lives. I taught group psychotherapy at Georgetown and worked with individuals, couples, families, and groups. The work was vibrant, meaningful, and deeply human.

But there were costs I had not anticipated. Sitting for hours each day contributed to degenerative spinal disease. More significantly, absorbing decades of emotional suffering — despair, rage, anxiety, marital turmoil, suicidal ideation — took a toll. To be a competent therapist, one must enter the patient's psyche, feel what they feel, and convey empathy without drowning in their pain. Mirror neuron research later confirmed what we intuitively knew: we reflexively absorb the emotional states of those before us. Forty years of doing so leave their mark.

Even with extensive personal analysis, our own frailties inevitably surface. We like to believe we take nothing personally, but we do. A patient's anger, despair, or idealization can stir deep countertransference. Sometimes the reaction is rooted in our past; sometimes it reflects an unconscious part of ourselves we would rather battle externally than confront internally. The line between realistic and transferential feelings is not always clear. In the intimate setting of therapy, even the illusion of falling in love can arise — a powerful positive transference that requires discipline, supervision, and self-scrutiny.

Many of my patients were high-functioning, emotionally generous individuals who enriched my life as much as I enriched theirs. But the full range of humanity — borderlines, acting-out adolescents, psychotics, sociopaths — made the work challenging. Practicing in the same community where I lived meant patients sometimes knew personal details about me, including my divorce and reluctance to remarry. Couples I treated for years would ask how I could teach relationship skills yet remain single. I told them I was still learning — slowly but surely.

Some patients were older and wiser than I was, with pedigrees from Oxford, Cambridge, and beyond. At times, I wondered why they were paying me instead of the other way around. I treated multiple generations within families — parents, children, grandchildren, even great-grandchildren. Group therapy, especially with video, was transformative. Seeing oneself on camera — the gestures, the tone, the unconscious signals — was revelatory. Mixing diverse individuals in a group created extraordinary breakthroughs.

For a period, I practiced out of a home office with a large stone fireplace. During snowstorms, groups would gather around the fire for marathon sessions. It felt like inviting friends into my home for evenings of honesty and confrontation. Those were the golden years of psychiatry — when we could treat mind, body, and spirit without interference.

Then came 1984. The Reagan administration slashed mental health coverage from unlimited sessions to fifty per year, then thirty. Insurance companies followed. My venerable analyst told me in a hardware store, "Psychoanalysis is dead." Managed care soon arrived, with young administrators instructing seasoned clinicians on how to treat patients from a manual. Psychiatrists became too expensive; social workers and psychologists were preferred. I joined one company briefly, regretted it, and withdrew.

I reduced my practice to three and a half days a week for fifteen years, working mostly with patients who did not rely on insurance. The role of medication dispenser — either alone or in collaboration with another therapist — was not one I enjoyed, but I adapted. Eventually, I began winding down, referring high-maintenance patients elsewhere, commuting monthly from Florida, and gradually weaning long-term patients over five years. After my final session, I spent five years as an expert medical witness before retiring fully.

Do I miss it? Yes and no. I miss the fulfillment of working with warm, intelligent, emotionally generous people. I do not miss the draining borderlines, sociopaths, and thieves — though they, too, taught me much. All professions have their costs. At times, I wished for objective tests — MRI, CT, PET — to clarify diagnoses rather than relying on clinical intuition. Psychiatry looks different today. Is it better? I think not.

Addendum: Despite occasional fantasies about dermatology, I have no regrets. It was a privilege to be trusted by so many extraordinary individuals willing to reveal their inner worlds. If I made a meaningful difference in their lives, then the toll — emotional, physical, and existential — was worth it.

GETTING BACK IN THE DRIVER'S SEAT

"Don't be yourself. Be a little nicer." — Mignon McLaughlin

There are times when we feel helpless, imprisoned by our own conditioned responses, as if we are no longer steering our lives but being steered by old, unconscious patterns. These reactions — shaped by childhood, family, culture, and temperament — can feel inescapable. We become Pavlovian creatures, responding reflexively, often primitively, in the hope of meeting our needs.

Most people remain trapped in these patterns for life. Others attempt to change them, with varying degrees of success, depending on motivation, capacity, and the chosen method.

My own training was traditional: slow, systematic, psychoanalytic. We listened to free associations, dreams, and slips of the tongue. We interpreted transference — the unconscious reenactment of past relationships in the present therapeutic encounter. This was the gold standard of the time, designed to dismantle resistance and cultivate maturity, peace of mind, and the capacity to love.

Though still practiced, classical analysis has largely faded from mainstream culture. Insurance companies refuse to reimburse it, and society demands quicker, outcome-oriented solutions. Many new approaches have emerged — some useful, others gimmicky. Psychoanalysis remains brilliant, but costly, time-consuming, and accessible only to those with the resources and motivation to commit. I was fortunate to undergo seven years of analysis, five days a week, at a time when insurance covered most of it.

One method that can accelerate therapeutic change is cognitive restructuring. Rather than excavating the origins of childhood, it focuses on revising the thought processes that trigger maladaptive emotional reactions. One of the most common interpersonal difficulties I've observed is the refusal to take responsibility for one's emotional responses. Instead of owning their reactions, people externalize — blaming others' words, actions, or imagined intentions. They become victims of external forces rather than agents of their own experience.

To counter this, I've found two cognitive principles particularly powerful. They place responsibility squarely where it belongs — on us — and restore a sense of agency:

1. **How someone feels about you at any given moment is a function of how you communicate with them.**
2. **How you feel about someone at any given moment is a function of the intention you ascribe to their words or behavior.**

In both cases, you are in the driver's seat. You decide how to communicate. You decide how to interpret. You choose whether to react or respond.

The first principle requires exquisite calibration — the ability to intuit what the other person needs to hear or experience to respond constructively. This demands presence, attentiveness, and flexibility. You gather information, remain attuned, and then communicate in a way that maximizes the likelihood of achieving your desired outcome. It is proactive rather than reactive.

Some people view this as manipulation — a con, a betrayal of authenticity, even sociopathic. But sociopaths hide their emotions to extract something from others. A healthy person modulates their reactions to create harmony, connection, and mutual well-being. Timing matters. Tone matters. Emotional maturity matters. Being "true to yourself" is not always virtuous if what you are expressing is unresolved childhood residue masquerading as honesty.

Think of this process as akin to being a skilled diplomat — someone who can hold back a knee-jerk reaction in the service of a greater good. It is not deceit; it is discipline. It is kindness. It is wisdom.

The second principle — how we interpret others' intentions — is equally transformative. We never truly know what someone is thinking. We guess. We speculate. We project. And often, we assume the worst. But if intention is always a guess, why not choose the interpretation that brings peace rather than turmoil?

Most people have no idea what drives their own behavior, let alone someone else's. We act, then retroactively construct explanations that sound plausible. These explanations become shared myths — comforting, coherent, and often wrong.

Since intention is always conjecture, why not create an interpretation that serves the relationship? Why not choose the meaning that fosters connection rather than conflict? The risk is minimal — being wrong — and the reward is substantial: harmony, warmth, and emotional safety.

Consider a man who feels upset because the woman he loves has become distant. His first interpretations may be catastrophic: she has another man, she's leaving, she no longer cares. These thoughts generate panic, anger, or despair. But if he pauses, breathes, and considers alternative intentions — she may be frightened, depressed, overwhelmed, or unsure of her entitlement to happiness — he can respond with patience and compassion rather than fear and accusation. The truth may emerge naturally, without chaos.

These two cognitive shifts — taking responsibility for how others feel about us and choosing the intention we ascribe to others — restore agency. They put us back in the driver's seat. They allow us to meet our needs without waiting for others to change. And they create an atmosphere of peace and love rather than conflict and helplessness.

This process also applies internally. Many people spend a lifetime believing their parents acted with malice, only to discover later — often after becoming parents themselves — that their parents were simply doing the best they could. Reinterpreting past intentions can lift decades of guilt, anger, and sadness. The truth matters less than the meaning that heals.

Some people cling to their negative interpretations as proof of their intelligence or insight. They would rather be right and miserable than wrong and happy. But happiness requires flexibility — the willingness to revise one's assumptions in service of emotional well-being.

In the end, these cognitive tools offer a path out of victimhood. They allow us to reclaim power, reduce suffering, and cultivate harmony. Life is short. Why not choose the interpretations and communications that bring joy rather than despair?

Addendum: Fine-tuning the mind with a few simple cognitive shifts can dramatically change how we experience life. These tools restore agency, reduce unnecessary suffering, and prevent us from becoming helpless puppets of our own conditioned reactions. Knowing that we can alter our interpretations — and thus our emotional lives — is a profound relief.

SOMETHING IN RETURN

"Parents who are afraid to put their foot down usually have children who step on their toes." — Chinese Proverb.

Being a parent is demanding work. It requires deep love, vigilance, and a sense of duty to meet a child's emotional and physical needs. Whether one parent is a couple, a single parent, or after a divorce, the responsibility remains the same: give what you can, within your capacity, so that the child grows into a mature, responsible adult. Parents with integrity strive to achieve this through a thoughtful balance of gratification and denial.

One concern I have — increasingly so — is the palpable sense of entitlement in many contemporary young adults. A significant number appear to have been overindulged, with the predictable consequence of becoming adults who struggle to support themselves. Even those who were not overindulged often feel deprived when comparing themselves to their more pampered peers. Entitlement spreads by contagion.

Where does this narcissistic entitlement originate? Does a child believe it is their birthright to receive unlimited support, regardless of what they give back? What does a parent truly owe a child — and does a child owe anything in return? Most human relationships thrive on mutuality. One-way streets breed resentment. Giving endlessly without receiving even basic respect or appreciation can feel depleting, even dehumanizing.

There is a saying: *"If you want to get everything you want from another, give them exactly what they want."* It sounds spiritual, noble, even enlightened — the promise that unconditional giving will inspire gratitude and reciprocity. But in my experience, both as a psychiatrist and as a father, it rarely works that way. Unconditional love is one thing; unconditional giving is quite another.

Parents who give endlessly may be afraid of rejection. They may fear abandonment or criticism and overindulge to avoid it. A perceptive child — especially one with a certain temperament — may sense this vulnerability and exploit it. They may feel guilty, but the cycle continues. The only way out is for the parent to pull back, set limits, and tolerate the child's temporary rage or withdrawal.

Sometimes withholding is more loving than giving. Constant indulgence can produce a spoiled, entitled adult who expects the world to operate like a personal concierge. The real world does not function that way. The spigot of abundance is not always open. *No good deed goes unpunished* often applies: the more a parent gives, the more they are taken for granted. The child may grow accustomed to abusing and disrespecting the parent with impunity — and this pattern often continues into adulthood, affecting partners, friends, and colleagues.

Parents who give less and who set limits often find that their children give more in return. Children must learn that rewards do not materialize simply because they exist; they must be earned through gratitude, respect, courtesy, or even simple acknowledgment.

I have heard countless parents say that the more they gave, the less they received, while those who gave in moderation were met with greater appreciation. One explanation may be developmental guilt. Children who sense they have been insensitive to their parents' needs may respond in one of two ways: they may become overly obedient, or they may double down on narcissistic behavior to avoid confronting their guilt. By continuing the mistreatment, they avoid facing the painful realization that they were wrong.

If a child recognizes that their parent did not deserve such treatment, remorse and sadness can follow — sometimes even depression. To avoid this discomfort, the tirades continue. A parent who absorbs this without setting limits only fuels the child's unconscious guilt. Limit-setting, deprivation, and consequences can actually reduce guilt and restore equilibrium. Parents who fail to do so often suffer ongoing retribution.

Both parent and child must feel secure enough to tolerate the inevitable frustrations of a relationship that oscillates between harmony and irritation. Expecting anything else is unrealistic.

In the end, parents do receive something in return — not only for the fulfillment of watching a child grow into a healthy adult, but also the respect, appreciation, and acknowledgment that come from balanced parenting. The key is avoiding both extremes: overindulgence and overrestriction. A thoughtful balance yields the best outcome — something meaningful in return for years of effort.

Addendum: Parenting is difficult. We learn through trial and error, often without ideal role models. Like navigating a boat with an imperfect chart, we discover where to go — and where not to go — through experience. I hope that by giving our best, we can eventually feel a sense of accomplishment, and that our children, as adults, will look back and agree.

SEVEN WORDS THAT KILL A RELATIONSHIP

"Honest, open communication is the only street that leads us into the real world... We then begin to grow as never before. And once we are on this road, happiness cannot be far away." — John Powell.

George Carlin had seven words you couldn't say on television. Mine are different — not profane, not taboo, not even unusual. They're ordinary, garden-variety words you hear every day. Yet they are deal breakers, the kiss of death for a relationship. You've probably uttered them yourself, unaware of their destructive power. And when the other person withdraws, shuts down, or disappears, you may find yourself bewildered — or, if you're honest, painfully aware of what you did but too proud to admit it.

Before revealing the seven words, let me lay the groundwork with a few examples.

After a dinner party, a friend — drunk and driving far too fast — refused my request to slow down or let me drive. He exploded: "If you don't like the way I drive, get the hell out and walk!" Silence followed. His wife screamed at him. I tried to talk it out. He said the seven words.

Another time, I was a houseguest, enjoying a fine Cuban cigar. My host stormed in, shouting, "Put that fucking cigar out!" I complied and asked, "What's going on with you?" He said the seven words.

I once suffered a severe financial loss, influenced in part by someone I cared for deeply. Whenever I tried to discuss it, she said the seven words.

On the golf course, a friend let two women play through without consulting the rest of our foursome. When I asked him to show us the courtesy of checking first, he grew defensive and angry. Several holes of silence later, he said, "I don't want to play golf with you anymore." I asked why. He said the seven words.

In each case, the rude behavior wasn't new — but the seven words marked the threshold. The door slammed shut. Without a sincere apology, remorse, or even minimal awareness, the relationship became untenable.

So, what are the infamous seven?

"I DON'T WANT TO TALK ABOUT IT."

Those words dismiss, devalue, and invalidate the other person's needs. They shut down the connection. They say, in effect: **Your feelings don't matter. Your experience doesn't matter. You don't matter.**

Add one word — *now* — and everything changes. "I don't want to talk about it **now**" implies postponement, not rejection. It buys time without destroying the bridge.

But the unqualified version? It's a relational guillotine.

Why do some people thrive on talking things out while others refuse? It's not gender-specific. I've heard both men and women shut down this way. Machismo men, afraid of vulnerability, and fiercely independent women who fear dependence, are especially prone to using the seven words. The result is the same: alienation, distance, and a relationship that becomes shallow, brittle, and devoid of intimacy.

Sometimes, there is enough good in the relationship to overlook the shutdown. Temporary circumstances may soften the blow. But if the issue festers, it must be reopened — debrided — or it will rot into resentment.

What drives the refusal to talk? Often, a fragile ego. The person may appear smug, self-righteous, or arrogant, but beneath the veneer lies terror — fear of criticism, fear of exposure, fear of shame. To admit fault feels like spiritual annihilation. They would rather be right and alone than wrong and connected.

Talking it out requires listening, learning, and acknowledging imperfection. It requires admitting that one may have misjudged, overreacted, or behaved insensitively. For some, this is intolerable. So, they flee into the seven words.

This pattern appears in children, adolescents, and immature adults — and in those with various psychiatric vulnerabilities. The refusal to talk is a defense against unbearable feelings.

In contrast, those who welcome dialogue gain clarity, insight, and growth. They see conversation not as humiliation but as an opportunity. Not everyone can process feelings instantly. Some need time. "I don't want to talk about it now" is legitimate — provided the delay is measured in hours, not days. Some delay in the hope that the issue will evaporate. It rarely does. A gentle reminder may be necessary.

Once someone experiences the benefits of healthy communication, the old pattern often dissolves. The brain learns the pleasure of resolution. The seven words lose their power. Relationships deepen. Self-esteem rises. Life becomes more meaningful. Survival mode gives way to connection.

The seas of life remain rough, but more navigable. Jumping into the ocean without knowing how to swim is foolish — yet many do it, armed only with the dysfunctional skills inherited from their parents. They pass these inefficiencies to their own children, perpetuating cycles of divorce, despair, and quiet desperation.

The origins of "I don't want to talk about it" become invisible, like water to a fish. We repeat what we learned without realizing how ineffective it is. Then, perhaps through therapy or a corrective emotional experience, we have an epiphany: the old way no longer works. It leads only to loneliness. The pain becomes too great. A shift occurs.

We stop saying the seven lethal words. We say instead: **"Let's talk about it."**

Addendum: Talking things out is the only way to work through the inevitable conflicts that arise in any relationship. Many long-married couples develop a "new normal," adapting to each other's quirks without ever truly communicating. But for those who are psychologically minded and emotionally attuned, avoiding the seven words is essential. It prevents relationships from devolving into quiet desperation, simmering resentment, or chronic ennui. The choice is ours.

YOU CAN'T PLEASE OR DISPLEASE ANYONE EVER

"You are not responsible for the programming you picked up in childhood. However, as an adult, you are one hundred percent responsible for fixing it." — Ken Keyes, Jr.

We have all experienced it countless times: that sting of disappointment, confusion, or disillusionment when someone disapproves of something we said or did. Some people love us, some dislike us, and some remain indifferent — often in response to the very same behavior. It leaves us bewildered, searching for explanations, and far too often, taking it personally.

The standard consolation we hear is, *"You can't please everyone."* Embedded in that phrase is the assumption that we could please everyone if only we tried hard enough — that we are somehow responsible for others' emotional reactions.

My contention is different, and for many, initially mind-bending: **You can't please or displease anyone — ever.** People please or displease themselves based on the internal filters through which they interpret the world.

Once you truly digest this, a remarkable relief follows. You stop worrying about how others respond to you. And just as importantly, you stop taking credit for the praise you receive. Their reactions — positive or negative — are reflections of *them*, not you.

I first grasped this concept at my 20th high school reunion. After seven years of psychoanalysis and years of psychiatric practice, I felt comfortable writing a deeply personal update for the reunion booklet. When I arrived, people had already read it.

Some approached me with warmth, saying how moved they were by my openness. Others asked if I had a compulsive need to expose myself — essentially calling me a horse's ass. During dinner, I flipped through the booklet. Those who praised my disclosure had written equally revealing entries. Those who criticized me had written almost nothing — some left their pages blank except for an address.

Later, when I received an award for "most explicit revelation," I made a brief speech: **"It appears that in defining me, who I am is at least as much a function of who you are. My disclosures simply triggered your stuff."**

Smiles and frowns escorted me off the stage. And I felt liberated. You can never please or displease anyone. People react according to their programming — their values, insecurities, histories, and emotional filters.

A child enters the world as a *tabula rasa*. Over time, environment, family, culture, and temperament shape their preferences, judgments, and knee-jerk reactions. By adulthood, each of us carries a unique internal program that determines what we value, reject, admire, or disdain.

This essay was prompted by a golf buddy's reaction to one of my more vulnerable pieces. I've been sharing my writing with various people to gauge potential readership. I knew exactly how he would respond — and he did not disappoint.

He is a classic macho, non-androgynous alpha male with a narrow range of interests: sports, business, women, movies, and — if I stretch it — politics. The subtleties of culture, literature, psychology, and emotional nuance lie far beneath his surface, if they exist at all.

After I read him an essay that had deeply touched many others, he said, "I don't know what to say. I have nothing to say." When I pressed him, he blurted, "You're fucked up!"

I laughed, called him a primitive clod, and told him to return to his gorilla cage. He laughed too and proudly told me "Gorilla" was his college nickname. "That doesn't make me a bad person, does it?" he asked.

I like this guy. He's a fun, warmhearted golf buddy. But psychologically, he's a lightweight. And from his frame of reference, *I'm* the one who's "fucked up."

If we hear the same reaction from many people, we may want to examine our stimulus value — if we prefer a different response. But in general, people react according to their programming. We can adjust our communication to evoke different responses, but ultimately, their reactions belong to them.

We are all different. Some people resonate with our worldview; others do not. Some become intimate companions; others remain golf buddies. Both have value. Being able to stay pleasant and connected — even when someone disapproves — is a worthy accomplishment. Knowing that their reaction has little to do with us can make all the difference.

Addendum: Staying grounded when someone thinks we're exceptional is as important as staying grounded when someone thinks we're awful. Neither reaction is truly about us. The world moves along on autopilot, with people reacting according to their internal programming. Trying to control their reactions is exhausting and futile. Better to observe, accept, and be grateful to still be standing on life's platform — or as my golf buddy would say, "Hey, you're on the right side of the grass, right?"

LET IT BE

"If you like it, let it be, and if you don't, please do the same." — Ani DiFranco.

I often imagine how peaceful and evolved we could be if we were able to simply take note of the human idiosyncrasies that collide with our own — to stand in their presence without emotional reactivity, without judgment, without the reflexive urge to correct or control. To "take note" is to observe another's words or behavior with a kind of Zen-like detachment, as if their actions had no power to disturb our equilibrium, even when they appear designed to shape us to fit their agenda.

There is tremendous power in non-reactivity. When we refuse to take the bait, we remove ourselves from the drama. The manipulative wind dies in their sails. Yet far too often, we hook ourselves into anxiety, guilt, anger, or sadness in response to someone else's attempts at need gratification — overt or covert.

As a psychiatrist, my instinct has long been to intervene, to use my training to ward off what I perceive as inappropriate behavior. But in doing so, I sometimes find myself engaging in the very dynamic I dislike — trying to change someone to fit my agenda of psychological health. I spent decades doing that in my office. I have no desire to continue doing it for free in my retirement.

The world is full of the "walking wounded," each performing their behavioral dance. Unless we retreat into total solitude, we inevitably encounter people who want us to operate differently — to give more, give less, be more attentive, be less independent, be more like the version of us they prefer.

Some of these individuals are, frankly, royal pains in the ass. Hence, this essay is an attempt to find a way to deal with them without losing my sanity or serenity.

"Control freaks" and "blemish collectors" are especially challenging. They scan the environment for flaws — in people, situations, objects — and then position themselves as the long-suffering victims of others' reactions to their criticism. When confronted, they often respond with, "I was only trying to help," as if their relentless fault-finding were an act of benevolence.

Pointing out their behavior gives me what I call the "therapeutic willies." I recoil from the impulse to correct them, even when their pattern is obvious. The repetition becomes exhausting, and sustaining a relationship with such a person becomes difficult. I find myself wondering whether it is possible to stay engaged without slipping into the role of unpaid therapist. I have no desire to provide corrective emotional experiences to people who neither recognize their issues nor seek help.

One particular individual brought this into sharp focus. Our relationship is platonic and activity-based, yet she often behaves as if I should treat her like a romantic partner — perhaps because she wishes it were so. She seems unable to register the many things I have done for her and focuses instead on what I have not done, as if she is entitled to more. Her disappointment is palpable. Her expectations are unspoken but unmistakable. And her rejection sensitivity — which she does not recognize — fuels the cycle.

She is vulnerable and dealing with significant health issues, and I have supported her as best I can. But I refuse to be depreciated for not fulfilling a fantasy role I neither want nor agreed to play. I have pointed out her controlling tendencies, but she cannot see them. Ironically, she once described her mother as critical and controlling — the resemblance is striking, though invisible to her.

This dynamic is not unique to her. It appears in anyone who lacks insight, curiosity, or the willingness to examine their interpersonal impact. With such individuals, depth becomes impossible; only superficial engagement remains tolerable.

Addendum: This brings me back to what I call the "Andy Warhol judgment call." Warhol could appreciate all forms of art — even the strange, the ugly, the bizarre. He collected them without discrimination. Can I reach a point where I can observe human quirks with the same neutrality? Can I remain calm as they bounce off me, silent and unperturbed, simply letting it be?

Perhaps I'll try that hat on for a while and see how many people assume I've had a lobotomy or early dementia. It would be a joy — and a relief — to achieve that level of equanimity. Let me add: I do not take any of these interactions personally. But being in the presence of such behavior is still unpleasant — reminiscent of a screeching monkey's distress call. And so, the practice continues: observe, detach, breathe, and let it be.

SWAGGERING MORTALITY

"I'm always described as cocksure or with a swagger, and that bears no resemblance to who I feel like inside. I feel plagued by insecurity." — Ben Affleck. *"Be kind, for everyone you meet is fighting a hard battle."* — Plato.

The other day at the health club, I noticed a middle-aged man with a pronounced swagger — the kind of strut that telegraphs smugness or self-importance. Yet I suspected that beneath the bravado lay something far more fragile.

His presence triggered an immediate negative reaction in me, one that felt unmistakably transferential. It reached back into childhood memories of bullies and arrogant narcissists — the boys who strutted through adolescence collecting the prettiest girls while the rest of us watched from the sidelines.

For a moment, I wondered whether my reaction contained a trace of envy or devaluation — a recognition that whatever swagger I once possessed has softened with age, as confidence inevitably shifts and recalibrates. I would have preferred, at this stage of life, to observe such a man with neutrality. But childhood has a way of haunting us long after we believe we've evolved beyond its reach.

My late psychoanalyst once told me that charisma — the genuine kind — fades with age. It is a healthier, more organic quality than swagger, though the two can coexist. Charisma is innate; swagger is compensatory. It is bravado, a façade. And while swagger can be adaptive — attracting partners in youth or projecting authority in adulthood — it becomes problematic when it eclipses empathy, when no one else seems to count but the swaggerer.

Consider the type of woman drawn to such a man. She often mirrors him — dramatic, insincere, strutting like a peacock. Both are engaged in the same desperate dance, using whatever assets they possess to meet their needs, however superficial those needs may be.

I once spoke with a patient about her style of relating to men. She said, "You've got to do what you can do with what you've got." She admitted she didn't score high in intellect or personality, but she knew her strengths — looks and sex appeal —, and she intended to capitalize on them. It was honest, if not entirely uplifting.

Swaggering males, strutting femmes fatales — these adaptations, however pitiful at times, serve a purpose. They generate a sense of confidence and self-esteem in an otherwise thorny existence. When viewed through this lens, the harshness of our reactions can soften. We begin to see the adaptive value rather than the superficial display.

Life is a grim struggle for most. In one way or another, we all cope with insecurity by employing mechanisms that may push others away rather than draw them in. Remembering this — along with the fleeting nature of the human condition — can soften our hearts. It allows us to reach out, even to the swaggering and strutting souls who seem least deserving of compassion.

Addendum: Why not give them the consideration they crave? Offer warmth to those who so desperately need it. Acknowledge their humanity. Beneath the bravado lies the same longing we all share — the need to be seen, understood, and loved.

HOPELESSLY LIVING IN HOPE

"Because what's worse than knowing you want something besides knowing you can never have it?" — James Patterson

Of all the forces that make life bearable, none is quite as essential as hope. With hope, we can relax, work, dream, and move forward in the face of adversity. Hope gives us something to look toward; without it, we feel sad, isolated, and unmoored. But hope must be realistic. When we cling to hope in situations that are, in truth, hopeless, the result is corrosive. We delude ourselves into believing that a person or circumstance will change, that the long-awaited shift will finally arrive and transform our well-being.

This pattern begins in childhood. As a survival mechanism, a child hopes that the selfish, indifferent, or cruel parent will one day become loving. The adult version of this drama is the partner who hopes the liar, cheater, or deceiver will finally reform — despite repeated assurances that never materialize.

On a broader scale, we see the same dynamic when a political figure promises sweeping transformation, charming and mesmerizing supporters with visions of miraculous change. When the results fall short, the disillusioned experience rage, impotence, and a sense of betrayal.

What kind of person inspires hope only to pull the rug out from under others? Sometimes it is a deeply troubled individual who derives satisfaction — consciously or unconsciously — from manipulating others into believing in them. This can stem from a malignant narcissistic impulse: the need to feel powerful rather than helpless, to dominate rather than risk vulnerability. It is a sadistic thrill — offering hope, then snatching it away.

More commonly, though, the dynamic arises from confusion, immaturity, or developmental impairment. These individuals lack the interpersonal depth required for healthy relationships. Their social skills are limited, their emotional communication impaired, and their sensitivity to others is minimal. They do not understand the basic relational requirement of taking responsibility for their actions and intentions. They react defensively, blame externally, and rarely self-examine.

Yet they may possess surface attributes — charm, attractiveness, financial success — that make them appealing. We overvalue these qualities and undervalue the essential prerequisites of a healthy relationship. By the time we recognize the deficit, the threshold has been crossed and the damage done.

Often, the person who becomes entangled with such an individual is desperate. My late mother had a Yiddish expression for this: *"A drowning man will grab hold of a razor blade."* In moments of need, we settle for far less than what is healthy. Later, we discover that not only did we waste precious time, but the emotional injury can be severe enough to impair trust and hinder future relationships.

Disillusionment after misplaced hope can lead to despair, withdrawal, and cynicism. But it can also spark an epiphany — a turning point that redirects one's life toward healthier choices. When hope collapses, clarity often emerges. We begin to prioritize sound judgment over desperation and to recognize the characterological criteria that truly matter.

Most people do not change without a radical life-altering event or a profound therapeutic experience. Surface qualities — generosity, wealth, charisma, sexual allure — are never enough. The real prerequisites include integrity, communication skills, empathy, gratitude, self-awareness, personal responsibility, kindness, consistency, fairness, the ability to love, the capacity for remorse, and the willingness to apologize.

None of these qualities exists without a grounded, well-esteemed sense of self.

As you review this checklist, remember Kenny Rogers' timeless advice: *"You've got to know when to hold 'em, know when to fold 'em, know when to walk away, and know when to run."* Whether at the card table or in life, those words are worth pondering.

Addendum: These essentials form the foundation of a healthy, durable relationship. When a leader — in any domain — lacks most of these attributes, the result is dysfunction. Hope all you want, but people rarely change in their later years. Their character is formed, their habits ingrained, their patterns predictable. Believing otherwise is not optimism; it is hopelessly living in hope.

MULTIPLE RELATIONSHIPS WITH ONE PERSON — A PREVENTIVE ANTIDOTE TO INFIDELITY

"Consistency is the last refuge of the unimaginative." — Oscar Wilde.

Infidelity — that perennial force that erodes the foundations of relationships — has plagued even those who take their commitments seriously. What appears to be irresponsible or immoral behavior often reflects deeper, unconscious dynamics. Human beings require emotional sustenance to thrive in a love relationship. When that nourishment fades, the yearning may surface elsewhere.

After the fact, we hear the familiar rationalizations: *"I was bored." "We were disconnected." "I felt unheard." "There was no affection, no passion."* These explanations appear to justify infidelity, though every long-term relationship contains some measure of boredom, anger, loneliness, or unmet needs. Psychological, biochemical, and genetic theories abound, each offering a piece of the puzzle. Here, I focus on one central dynamic — and one possible antidote.

Traditionally, infidelity was thought to be more common among men. That may once have been true, but with more women in the workplace and living autonomous lives, the balance has shifted. In my psychiatric practice, I've heard countless women describe their affairs with candor and complexity. Romantic longing often drives women, while men more frequently operate from instinctual, hormonal impulses — though the reverse certainly occurs.

The film *Unfaithful* illustrates this shift. Diane Lane's character, Connie Sumner, has a seemingly perfect life, yet engages in an affair with a younger man. Boredom? Too much time? Perhaps. But the deeper message is that women, too, have begun to use youthful lovers as men historically have — not out of necessity, but because they can.

Some argue that men are genetically predisposed to adultery — an evolutionary imperative to propagate their seed. Feminists often dismiss this as male propaganda. But another explanation resonates more deeply with me: **the fear of death**.

In *Moonstruck*, Rose Castorini asks, "Why do men chase women?" Perry answers, "We're afraid of death." Rose replies, "Right." It's a deceptively simple exchange — and profoundly true.

Long-term relationships can become stagnant, predictable, or even deadened. Some describe marriage as "the last nail in the coffin of life." The unconscious mind equates stagnation with death. In youth, we are in constant motion — running, dancing, exploring. As we age, we retreat into familiarity, safety, and routine. Life becomes calmer but loses its sparkle. Movement slows. Mood dims. The Grim Reaper whispers.

Infidelity, then, becomes a misguided attempt to feel alive — an adrenaline-fueled denial of mortality.

In *My Dinner with Andre*, Andre Gregory says, "By being committed and monogamous and vulnerable to my wife Chiquita, I feel frightened when I look into her eyes knowing she will probably be the last person to see me before I die." Commitment brings love — and vulnerability. Avoiding commitment brings the illusion of immortality — at a steep price.

Affair after affair offers temporary vitality, but eventually one wakes up alone, time having run out, with no meaningful shoulder to cry on.

Most of us live far beneath our potential. Unless we undergo deep psychoanalysis or experience a profound emotional breakthrough, we present ourselves predictably — a small slice of who we truly are. Predictability offers comfort, but too much of it breeds boredom. Adventure stimulates, but too much of it becomes chaotic. Each of us requires a unique balance.

We are multi-layered beings, yet most of us avoid exploring the undiscovered crevasses of our inner world. E.E. Cummings wrote, *"It takes courage to grow up and turn out to be who we really are."* Our public selves are shaped by years of conditioning. How much of our essential core remains undeveloped is impossible to know.

But while time remains, we can choose to awaken dormant parts of ourselves — to become more multifaceted, more alive, more interesting to ourselves and our partners. These hidden aspects — wit, passion, depth, playfulness — lie within us, waiting to be expressed.

For those who value predictability above all else, this may sound unsettling. But every dream, fantasy, and experience we've ever had resides within our psyche and our genetic lineage. Accessing them requires trust — the willingness to reveal new parts of ourselves without fear of looking foolish.

Expressing these new aspects can be both exhilarating and risky. Some people prefer the familiar version of us and may try to pull us back into old patterns. They may interpret our growth as instability rather than expansion. Early expressions of new parts may be raw, even awkward, until they settle into authenticity. But once pretension falls away, the relief is immense. Authenticity requires far less effort than maintaining a façade.

This process demands flexibility, creativity, and the ability to recognize and accept internal contradictions. We must acknowledge that we contain the full spectrum of human qualities — good and bad, moral and immoral, dominant and vulnerable, selfless and selfish. Integrating these contradictions creates wholeness.

Some people access these parts through psychedelics or alcohol — one reason such substances are so popular. But it is far healthier to do so without chemical assistance.

When partners discover and celebrate new facets of each other — more humor, more depth, more passion — the relationship becomes an adventure. Boredom evaporates. Vitality returns. Death feels less threatening. And infidelity becomes unnecessary.

Addendum: Skeptics may dismiss this approach as fanciful. But beliefs are not about truth; they are about usefulness. Would you rather cling to old beliefs and remain miserable, or adopt a new understanding and risk being happily wrong? The question is not which belief is "correct," but which belief produces the life you want. As with faith in God, if peace of mind matters, the belief itself can be transformative.

Is it possible to have multiple relationships with one person — to continually rediscover each other — as an antidote to infidelity? Believe what you wish. The proof lies in the creative outcome.

ON INFIDELITY

"When love becomes labored, we welcome an act of infidelity toward ourselves to free us from fidelity." — François de La Rochefoucauld.

Infidelity has shadowed intimate relationships for as long as relationships have existed. After decades in psychiatry, I've heard every imaginable justification — from the tortured to the absurd. Some people claim they have no idea what drove them; most create a narrative that makes perfect sense to them. I've seen people in seemingly ideal marriages stray, others remain faithful but live in fantasy, and still others insist they never desired anyone but their partner.

Some argue that infidelity is a myth — a social invention designed to preserve the family unit. In the animal kingdom, monogamy is the exception, not the rule. Without moral and religious structures, humans might simply follow instinctual urges, with predictable chaos. Cultural norms, community size, and fear of exposure all influence how tightly people adhere to monogamy.

But instinct alone doesn't explain infidelity. Genetics, temperament, risk-taking tendencies, and early conditioning all play a role. Some people are wired for thrill and novelty; others are cautious and reflective. Some act impulsively; others agonize over consequences. The origins are complex, but certain patterns recur.

ETIOLOGIES OF INFIDELITY (Condensed)

Hedging Against Vulnerability

Some people cannot tolerate the risk of being hurt. They strike first — cheating to avoid being cheated on — and in doing so, avoid true intimacy altogether.

Greed and Entitlement

Those raised with overindulgence or deprivation may grow into adults who believe they deserve "everything." When their partner inevitably disappoints, they seek someone new to restore their fragile self-esteem.

Validation and Aging

As beauty fades or attention shifts elsewhere, some panic. Cosmetic fixes, flirtation, and affairs become desperate attempts to reclaim lost desirability — physical or otherwise.

Retaliation

The unconscious mind loves symmetry. When wounded, some seek revenge. A retaliatory affair can temporarily restore a damaged ego, though it often deepens the rupture.

Dependency and Loneliness

An absent or overworked partner leaves a void. Someone attentive appears, and the emotional hunger becomes too great to resist.

Identification with an Unfaithful Parent

Children absorb what they witness. Growing up around deceit normalizes it, and the script repeats in adulthood.

Hormonal and Biochemical Drives

Youth, mania, impulsiveness, and high libido can push some toward multiple partners. For others, fantasy suffices; for some, action becomes irresistible.

Acting Out Instead of Talking Out

Those raised in non-communicative families may express conflict through behavior rather than words. Affairs become emotional language.

Substance-Induced Disinhibition

Alcohol and drugs lower inhibitions and provide a convenient alibi: "I was too drunk to know better."

Marrying for the Wrong Reasons

Security, status, or convenience cannot sustain emotional fulfillment. The heart eventually seeks what it lacks.

Chronic Emptiness

Those with deep emotional voids may pursue affairs to soothe infantile needs that no partner can satisfy.

Contempt for the Opposite Sex

Some reenact childhood trauma by proving that all men or women are untrustworthy — seducing others simply to confirm their worldview.

The Oedipal Drama

Unresolved childhood longing for the unavailable parent can lead to lifelong pursuit of forbidden partners.

The Obsessive Collector

For some, sexual experiences become trophies — a compulsive quest with no endpoint.

Bohemian Experimentation

Open marriages and communal arrangements often collapse under the weight of human jealousy and longing.

Altruistic Infidelity

Occasionally, a partner encourages an affair out of compassion, age, illness, or incapacity, prompting a selfless gesture.

Platonic Escalation

Friendship deepens, emotional intimacy grows, and the line between connection and romance blurs.

Cultural Sanctioning

The media glamorizes affairs, making them appear exciting, sophisticated, or inevitable.

Sexual Addiction

For some, the pursuit of novelty becomes compulsive — a narcotic against emptiness.

End-Stage Relationships

When love has long died, an affair becomes a lifeline in an otherwise barren emotional landscape.

Fear of Intimacy

True intimacy requires vulnerability. Affairs create distance and preserve emotional safety.

The New Woman

With shifting gender roles and economic independence, women now stray at rates comparable to men.

Married Too Young

Those who never explored their autonomy may later feel compelled to "catch up."

Ambitious Couples

Exhaustion, stress, and lack of intimacy create fertile ground for temptation.

Swingers and Sexual Adventurers

Eventually, novelty wears thin, and emptiness sets in.

Searching for Nirvana

Some chase the illusion of "more, different, better," never realizing that peace comes from wanting what one has.

Physicality and Sexual Magnetism

Attraction and great sex can masquerade as love — until reality intrudes.

Romance Junkies

Those addicted to the high of early love seek new partners when the initial rush fades.

Different Love Languages

Partners who cannot understand each other's emotional language may feel unloved and look elsewhere.

The Familiar Family

As partners become "family," sexual energy diminishes. Strangers feel excited because they allow us to be new versions of ourselves.

Envy and Triangles

Some can only feel desire when competing with another. The triangle becomes the fuel.

Forbidden Passion

Breaking taboos creates intensity. Danger becomes the aphrodisiac.

Self-Punishment

Some sabotage happiness out of guilt, unworthiness, or unconscious loyalty to parental misery.

Masochistic Dynamics

Affairs that guarantee suffering — jealousy, fear, comparison — become a form of emotional self-harm.

Power and Triumph

Some reenact childhood helplessness by orchestrating adult scenarios where they "win."

Married and Suddenly Desirable

Commitment signals value: others want what someone else has chosen.

Jealousy as Foreplay

For some couples, insecurity fuels passion. The cycle is volatile but intoxicating.

PREVENTION AND TREATMENT

Preventing infidelity depends on who the individuals are — psychologically, culturally, and developmentally. Clergy, therapists, and self-help resources can all play a role, but professional guidance accelerates growth. Relationship skills are learned, not innate. Unless we were raised by emotionally healthy parents — a rare privilege — we inherit dysfunctional patterns that require conscious effort to unlearn.

Breaking generational scripts takes time, discipline, and humility. There are no shortcuts.

Addendum: A recurring theme in my writing is my hesitation to remarry. I've had many meaningful relationships, yet the fear of infidelity remains one of the most potent barriers. After decades of treating couples devastated by betrayal, I know how deep the wounds can go.

Writing this essay is my attempt to understand, prepare, and perhaps one day take the risk again. But I suspect that no amount of intellectual preparation can fully protect the heart. When love arrives, the leap is emotional, not analytical — and the vulnerability is the price of admission.

PROTECT THEM FROM SUICIDE

"Every creature is better alive than dead... and he who understands it aright will rather preserve its life than destroy it." — Henry David Thoreau.

While watching a *20/20* segment on suicides at the Golden Gate Bridge, I was struck by the stark footage of people leaping to their deaths — and by the project's goal: to show that suicide is preventable. The program ended with a discussion about constructing barriers to stop the twenty-plus annual jumpers.

Immediately afterward, *20/20* pivoted to a light piece on food packaging and overeating. The contrast was jarring. Yet the juxtaposition revealed something important: both segments addressed self-destructive behavior — one dramatic and visible, the other subtle and socially sanctioned.

The next morning, I found myself thinking about a former ballerina I know — a woman compelled to under-eat and over-exercise. She had watched the same program, then went to bed early so she could rise before dawn for the first of her two daily spinning classes. For those unfamiliar, spinning can burn nearly a thousand calories an hour. She consumes perhaps 300–500 calories a day. At five foot six, she weighs ninety-odd pounds; her healthy weight would be 115–120. Any attempt to gain even a few pounds fills her with dread.

Thomas Szasz, the libertarian psychiatrist, famously argued that people have the right to destroy themselves and that society has no business intervening. I never subscribed to that view. Yet many health clubs — consciously or not — seem to operate under Szasz's philosophy. Some express concern and ask her to slow down. Others praise her endurance, oblivious to the danger. A few may even encourage her because her compulsive attendance is good for business.

She is a gifted athlete, a former American Ballet Theatre dancer, and her cardiovascular conditioning is extraordinary. But she is also in peril. She cannot protect herself. She needs others to step in before she collapses under a defibrillator in some well-meaning gym.

Eating disorders and compulsive over-exercise are rampant. Just as the Golden Gate Bridge needs a guardrail, health clubs need staff trained to recognize when a member is spiraling toward self-harm. And Dr. Szasz, wherever you are, society has moved beyond your 1960s insistence on absolute non-interference.

A moral society protects those who cannot protect themselves — just as we would stop a toddler or a puppy from running into traffic. Yes, personal freedom matters. Yes, we recoil at the idea of Big Brother monitoring our choices. But there is a difference between policing people and preventing tragedy.

Imagine grabbing someone by the shoulders as they lean over the Golden Gate railing. Maybe they will jump another day. But at that moment, you bought them time — time to reconsider, time to breathe, time to live. Sometimes that is enough.

Addendum: I feel deeply about our responsibility to one another. I am continually shocked by how many people look away, unwilling to intervene even when a life is visibly unraveling. Perhaps we all need to ask ourselves what stops us from stepping in — fear, apathy, discomfort, or the illusion that "it's not our business." If we can overcome that hesitation, we may save someone who cannot save themselves. And if nothing else, we will sleep better knowing we tried.

MY BALLERINA

"The heart has its reasons of which reason knows nothing." — Blaise Pascal.

Never in my wildest imaginings did I expect the relationship I found myself in. One might assume that, in the September of my years, I would drift into a gentle companionship with an age-appropriate woman — someone with grown children, a love of travel, a shared interest in golf, and a calming presence for the final chapters of life. But life, as it often does, had other plans.

It began on an ordinary morning at the health club. While on the elliptical, I noticed a thin, attractive blonde on the adjacent machine, exercising with fierce intensity while reading *The New York Times*. Her posture was impeccable — elongated neck, hair pulled tight into a ponytail, movements precise and graceful. She looked like a bookish librarian at first glance, but the carriage of her body suggested something else.

"Excuse me," I asked, "are you a professional dancer? A ballerina?" She turned, surprised. "Yes, as a matter of fact, I am." "Were you with a company?" "The American Ballet Theatre."

I felt a small thrill of diagnostic pride — and then promptly ruined it by blurting out, "Are you also anorectic?" She stared at me, startled. "Are you a psychiatrist?" "Yes," I admitted.

The rest of the conversation is a blur, but I remember her intelligence, sophistication, and the rare pleasure of speaking with someone who understood nuance — not just linguistically, but philosophically and emotionally. She was Manhattan, Boston, Washington — not Miami. A Brearley girl, a Professional Children's School alumna, a Harvard graduate, raised on the Upper East Side. She was the world I had left behind.

At the time, she was thirty-six; I was sixty-four. I expected nothing beyond friendship. But she called, asked me out, and something in me stirred — flattered, curious, alive. I had just ended a relationship with a young Latina who had many virtues but could not meet me intellectually. With the ballerina, conversation itself became intimacy.

As our connection deepened, so did the relationship. Her gentleness, grace, and sensuality helped me recover from the emotional blow of prostate surgery. Her sensitivity, however, cut both ways. She felt everything too intensely — taking blame for what wasn't hers, projecting blame when it was clearly hers. She was exquisitely compassionate and exquisitely wounded.

She needed help, but I could not ethically or effectively provide it. I recommended one of Manhattan's finest psychoanalysts — a *New York Times*–profiled, world-class clinician. She refused. She had endured more loss than most: her mother at twelve, her brother recently, and her beloved father not long before we met. Exercise and starvation became her coping mechanisms — the familiar, deadly duet of anorexia nervosa.

She spent six to eight hours a day exercising, consuming barely enough calories to sustain life. I watched her shrink — physically, emotionally, existentially. She cycled through health clubs, each one alarmed and asking her to stop. She promised to enter a six-week inpatient program, stayed two, and fled.

And yet she was extraordinary. Brilliant. Curious. A classical pianist who refused to play. A ballerina who refused to dance. A woman of privilege who despised possessions and lived as a minimalist. A voracious reader who devoured the *Times* and multiple books a week. A mind that challenged and enriched mine.

But she could not live a normal life. She would not travel except for brief trips to New York. She rarely slept over. She adhered to a rigid routine that left little room for companionship. And still — she was there for me in emergencies, loving and supportive in ways that mattered.

We broke up and reunited countless times. I could not leave. I loved her — deeply, irrationally, helplessly. And how does one abandon someone who has been abandoned by everyone else?

My family and friends urged me to move on. They saw how she constricted my social life, my spontaneity, my desire for shared adventures. But she was irreplaceable. My ninety-nine-year-old mother asked, "You love this woman, don't you?" "Yes, Mom. I do."

The question became unavoidable: Can I afford the emotional price of loving someone who cannot fully show up? No social life. No travel. No shared daily companionship. Only the slivers of time she could spare between compulsive workouts. The honest answer was no — unless she made significant changes. She could not. Or would not.

She often told me to find a healthier woman. When I finally began dating, she was devastated. "Why encourage me," I asked, "only to beg me not to?" "I'm confused," she said.

She has since withdrawn. Weeks have passed without contact. I can only hope for an epiphany — a shift that brings us back together in a healthier place. I miss her. I will always love her. She is unforgettable.

Addendum: It is a particular sorrow to love someone who cannot offer the commitment you believe you want. At times, I wonder whether I am drawn only to those who cannot "close the deal," or whether I, too, would falter if they could. I may never know. Her eating disorder — that unwelcome, unyielding intruder — has been the true third partner in our relationship, and it has always had the final say.

THE LURE OF THE VULNERABLE WOMAN

"Do not bite at the bait of pleasure until you know there is no hook beneath it."
— Thomas Jefferson. *"Women are never stronger than when they arm themselves
with their weakness."* — Marquise du Deffand.

I've been thinking a great deal about my avoidance of remarriage and
my tendency to choose women who, for one reason or another, give
me a justifiable exit ramp. I wonder whether the pattern lies not in the
women themselves but in the kind of woman I am drawn to — and
what that attraction reveals.

What makes these women so appealing? On the surface, they look like
anyone else. But look more closely: their eyes, their posture, the way
they speak. They are open, exposed, undefended. Their armor is thin.
They radiate a softness that awakens something archetypal in a man
— the impulse to protect, rescue, and shelter.

By contrast, the less vulnerable woman is more defended, more self-
contained, less trusting. She reveals little. Her emotional underbelly is
hidden. And while I admire her strength, I do not fall in love with her.
I cannot cry in front of her. I cannot be fully myself.

Some people respond to "How are you?" with a breezy "Everything's
great!" — as if emotional disclosure were a foreign language. They
skim the surface of life, offering social niceties instead of substance.
With them, intimacy feels impossible. Estrangement is built into the
structure.

As a young man, I was drawn to actresses like Natalie Wood, Jean
Simmons, and Kim Novak — women whose screen presence carried a
trace of childhood injury. Their vulnerability was palpable. Others,
equally talented and beautiful — Lauren Bacall, Jane Russell, Ava
Gardner — projected a harder shell. Admirable, yes. But not the ones
who stirred my heart.

These traits appear early in life. Some women grow into assertive, take-charge personalities, often pairing with less assertive men who feel comfortable with their strength. I respect these women deeply — but I do not fall in love with them. My wiring seems to require the magnetic pull of vulnerability.

When I think of the few times, I've truly been in love, a common thread emerges: I felt safe enough to express the full range of my emotions — including the kind of crying that empties a box of tissues. To be raw, naked, undefended, and still loved. Without that, love feels like a fantasy rather than a reality.

The vulnerable woman also tends to embrace the strong male lead — in sex, in dance, in life. She yields, not out of weakness, but out of trust. Her softness allows the man to feel strong. And once he feels secure, he can relax and let her lead when she wishes. No power struggle. No tug of war. Just a smooth, harmonious dance.

For some couples, conflict is foreplay. For me, it is friction. I prefer the synchronous rhythm of mutual compatibility.

The more I examine this attraction, the more I see that the vulnerable woman offers something beyond romance: a refuge. A sanctuary. A place to land when life becomes overwhelming. It is hard to know how universal this is among men, whether it is archetypal or rooted in childhood experience. But for men with wounded inner boys, the soft woman is the antidote to danger.

My mother — like many women of her generation — lived in survival mode. Vulnerability was hidden behind criticism and control. Nurturing was scarce. Comfort was conditional. It is easy to see how the vulnerable woman became, for me, a corrective emotional experience — a chance to rewrite the past.

But here is the trap: **I cannot cure her any more than I can cure my childhood.** And yet I have tried — repeatedly. I have chosen women who needed rescuing, believing that if I could heal them, I could heal myself. But they remained unchanged, and I eventually left — relieved but also repeating the old script of escape.

To break the pattern, I must stay. I must tolerate criticism without collapsing. As my psychoanalyst once said, "Take the punch, Jack. It won't kill you." But the slightest expression of anger from a woman — reminiscent of my mother — has historically sent me running.

It is also possible that by choosing vulnerable women, I have protected myself from confronting my own abandonment issues. Their dependency shielded me from the deeper terror of being left by someone strong and self-possessed.

It is time to spend more time with women who do not immediately expose their hands. To tolerate their coolness without recoiling. To trust that their vulnerability exists — just beneath the surface — and will emerge in time.

Writing this essay has been an attempt to understand the impediments that have kept me from creating a lifelong intimate relationship. My staying power has historically been five to seven years. I never know where the writing will take me, but the word "lure" should have been a clue: the vulnerable woman is the bait, and I am the fish who keeps biting.

Addendum: Time is running down. For whatever years remain, it makes sense to choose a good woman who can be a constant. I must lay my childhood ghosts to rest and venture into unfamiliar territory — toward women who do not rely on vulnerability as their calling card. I know, deep down, that I have outgrown the lure. Smooth and seductive at first, the hook is always there. Without the decoy, I am free to explore the full body of water — and trust that the right woman will reflect everything I have become.

PREDATORY MEN AND THEIR JUST DESSERTS

"The first woman was created from the rib of a man... out of his side to be equal to him." — Confucius.

I'm no kid anymore. I've lived long enough to have seen fashions, presidents, and libidos rise and fall — sometimes in the same decade. And yet, like so many men I know, I'm still struck by how persistent the male fascination with female sexuality remains. You'd think that after enough years, heartbreak, and prostate exams, the obsession would fade. It doesn't. Most men seem wired with a lifelong magnetism toward the erotic — a kind of ancient homing device that never fully powers down.

Where does this come from? Long before puberty, boys are already captivated by the mystery of the feminine. And long after testosterone has taken a nosedive, the fascination lingers like a stubborn houseguest. It's as if biology installed a program we can't uninstall, no matter how many birthdays we've celebrated.

Of course, not all men are wired the same way. Some have minimal interest in sexual pursuit, whether due to temperament, biology, or psychological inhibition. But for the majority, the attraction is powerful enough to fuel entire industries — from pornography to advertising to the endless parade of sexualized imagery that saturates modern culture. If desire were a stock, it would never dip below a strong buy.

One might assume that with the internet's endless supply of explicit content, men would eventually become numb. In the 1970s, when pornographic films flooded theaters, the novelty wore off quickly. But despite the saturation, the fascination persists. Desire is stubborn. It adapts. It finds new outlets. It's the Houdini of human drives.

During the sexual revolution — before HIV reshaped the landscape — promiscuity became almost recreational. Then came the backlash, the fear, the moral recalibration. Yet even with new restraints, men remained captivated by what I'll call, for lack of a better term, **female erotic power**.

For generations, men were unsubtle about their desires, while women were expected to keep theirs hidden. But that dynamic has shifted dramatically. Today's women, empowered by feminism, reproductive autonomy, and cultural permission, have become far more open about their own sexual appetites. They objectify men with the same unapologetic gusto men once reserved for women. Think of the Chippendales phenomenon, or the explosion of devices and technologies designed to bypass male participation entirely.

In many ways, men are now getting their just desserts. Women are making it abundantly clear that they do not need men for sexual fulfillment — and that the male body can be objectified just as easily as the female one. The message is unmistakable: *We can play this game too.*

And here's the philosophical twist: When the pendulum swings far enough in either direction, it eventually forces a reckoning. Men, stripped of their old sexual dominance, may finally have to show up differently — as equals, as friends, as human beings with emotional depth rather than as walking embodiments of desire. Women, having claimed their autonomy, may meet men on more balanced ground. Perhaps this mutual unmasking will lead to something healthier than the old scripts ever allowed.

The memoir piece? I've lived long enough to see the entire arc — from the days when men strutted like roosters to the present era where women have reclaimed their own erotic agency. And I've watched men, me included, slowly realize that the old model was never sustainable. Lust alone is a flimsy foundation for anything meaningful. It burns hot, then burns out.

Genuine affection grows not from objectification but from curiosity, respect, and shared humanity. The sexual revolution and the feminist movement both overshot their marks at times — as all revolutions do.

But overshooting is often part of the process. Eventually, we recalibrate. Men and women need to make peace with each other, to celebrate differences without exploiting them, and to recognize that sexuality divorced from emotional connection leads to emptiness, not fulfillment.

Desire will always exist. Attraction will always be powerful. But if we can integrate those forces with empathy and respect, we may finally arrive at a culture where neither gender is reduced to anatomy nor utility.

Addendum: Yes, men have gotten their just desserts. Whether this reckoning will lead to a healthier cultural balance remains to be seen. Only hindsight — the retro-periscope — will tell us whether this era has brought us closer together or pushed us further apart. I hope we land somewhere in the middle — where desire is still alive, but no longer the only language men and women speak.

A STRANGE REUNION

"Love that we cannot have is the one that lasts the longest, hurts the deepest, and feels the strongest." — Kay Knudsen.

Joe Louis once said of his opponents, "He can run, but he can't hide." In today's world, that line applies far more broadly. The social-media revolution has made anonymity nearly impossible. Facebook, LinkedIn, Instagram, Google — they've turned the world into a searchable archive of our lives. What once required detective work now takes seconds. We live in an era of voluntary exposure, part networking tool, part narcissistic theater.

For better or worse, anyone from our past can find us. Sometimes the result is a delightful surprise — a chance to reconnect, repair, or rediscover. Other times, it's a reopening of wounds that were better left sealed.

A successful reunion requires two people who have resolved enough of their old emotional debris to meet as adults. But some remain stuck in fear, anger, or grief, unable to risk vulnerability even decades later.

A woman I once loved — deeply, painfully — found me this way. She was twenty-two when we met; I was twenty-eight. After reading a condensed version of a personal article I'd published, she Googled me and reached out through a social network. I was surprised, touched, and cautiously hopeful.

She asked about my life; I asked about hers. But her responses were partial, guarded. I had revealed much; she revealed little. I respected her caution, wanting nothing more than a warm, human exchange after so many years. Still, I sensed her ambivalence — the push-pull dynamic I remembered all too well.

I wondered whether I had asked something too intimate. Perhaps inquiring about her husband's and son's health felt intrusive. Or perhaps the mere act of reconnecting with a man she once loved felt disloyal within the context of her marriage.

It wasn't the first time. Twenty-five years earlier, she had resurfaced, reached out, then abruptly vanished. And before that — in 1972 — she flew to Washington, D.C., arriving with a dozen red roses. I was hopeful, open, ready. But by the end of the weekend, she pushed me away again. I was blindsided. Heartbroken. Confused.

Looking back, I now see the pattern: her ambivalence, her fear, her unfinished business. And perhaps my own. At the time, I told myself I left her because I was too close to my divorce. But maybe my intuition was sharper than I realized. Maybe I sensed even then that she would be a difficult partner — loving, yes, but conflicted, mistrustful, and emotionally volatile.

For years, I idealized her as "the one who got away." Social media, ironically, gave me the chance to finally lay that myth to rest.

But then something shifted. Our emails grew warmer, more intimate, more honest. Her reluctance softened. Mine did too. Eventually, we agreed to meet the next time I was in New York.

The rendezvous was set for the steps of the Metropolitan Museum of Art. She told me I'd recognize her by the breed of dog she'd be walking. I spotted her instantly. I approached from behind, put my arms around her, and said, "You look just like a gal I very much loved forty years ago." She turned, startled, smiling.

It was 9 a.m. The day evaporated. We talked, laughed, touched, and reminisced. The connection — astonishingly — was still there. Not as nostalgia, but as something alive. Something that had waited.

I don't know what she felt. But for me, it was exquisite — a rare, almost surreal blend of past and present. She was, in many ways, the closest thing I've ever had to a soul mate. And perhaps always will be.

But reality remains. She is married to a good man. She lives in New York; I live in Key Biscayne. She introduced me to her son as an old friend. Could she do the same with her husband? I don't know. I told her I would visit her home next time I was in the city. I meant it. And I meant it when I told myself I would maintain boundaries. I am capable of being a friend to a woman I care for — even one I once loved.

If circumstances change, perhaps the door opens. If not, I can still honor what we shared.

Addendum: Can two people who once loved each other, break apart painfully, and live entire lives in between, reunite and thrive? Sometimes yes. Often no. My intuition tells me that most attempts to resurrect old relationships end in disappointment. And yet — even if this ends here — I am grateful. In a short life, moments like this are rare: a strange, beautiful fusion of now and then, a reminder that some connections never fully die, even if they cannot fully live.

REUNITING WITH THE PAST

"There is a way to look at the past. Don't hide from it. It will not catch you if you don't repeat it." — Pearl Bailey.

There are moments when I imagine having a time machine — the H.G. Wells kind — to revisit the romantic crossroads of my life and see whether I could have done things differently. The question isn't about blame; it's about curiosity. Were the relationships that failed truly doomed, or was I simply too young, too reactive, too unformed to make them work?

With age comes the illusion of growth — and perhaps some real growth too. So, it seems only fair to wonder whether the man I am now would have chosen differently, or stayed longer, with the women I once loved.

The closest thing we have to a time machine is Facebook. Type in a name, or have someone type in yours, and suddenly you're back in contact after fifty years. It's astonishing. Loose ends can be tied. Old questions can be answered. And sometimes, long-buried feelings resurface.

Some former partners are happily married, others not so much. Some are divorced, some are single, some still searching. I've reconnected with a few — cautiously — guided by intuition. And it's remarkable how quickly the old vibe returns. The same energy that once drew me in or pushed me away reappears instantly, as if no time has passed at all.

It's easy, with distance, to idealize "the one who got away." To mourn what might have been. But spending time with a former girlfriend decades later can be profoundly clarifying. You realize, often within minutes, that your original decision to leave was correct. The same incompatibility reemerges. The same emotional patterns. The same reasons you couldn't commit then — they're still there now, only more pronounced.

If anything, age lowers the tolerance threshold. With so little time left, who wants to spend precious hours with someone who doesn't move your soul? Life requires tolerance, yes, but not at the cost of daily irritation or emotional depletion. Some quirks are manageable; others are deal breakers. And the older you get, the clearer the distinction becomes.

Looking back, I sometimes marvel at what young adults will endure in the name of sexual chemistry. Passion acts like a biochemical tranquilizer — muting irritability, smoothing over incompatibilities, creating the illusion of harmony. Remove the sexual glue, and what remains is companionship. A very different equation.

As a mature adult, you move more slowly. You ask whether the connection is worth pursuing. In youth, you leap first and question later — if at all.

So along comes Facebook, offering a second look. And almost always, what shows up is confirmation: you were right to leave. The fantasy dissolves. The obsessive "what ifs" evaporate. You see the past clearly, without the haze of longing or regret.

Addendum: Our intuitive mind — that quiet, unconscious compass — often protects us better than we realize. Sometimes being alone is simply another form of not being alone. When the right person appears, the choice will feel natural. I hope that happens before rigor mortis sets in. Ending this glorious life with a well-matched partner seems preferable, though not essential. I'll give it my best shot — but not through the Facebook time machine.

BECOMING PHYSICALLY INTIMATE — SOONER OR LATER

"Use, do not abuse; neither abstinence nor excess ever renders a man happy." — Voltaire.

When we're young, hormones behave like overcaffeinated personal trainers — barking orders, pushing us forward, and drowning out any whisper of reason. We leap into physical intimacy with the enthusiasm of someone jumping into a cold pool without checking the depth. The genetic imperative to procreate overrides caution, reflection, and common sense. Lust becomes the engine, and love — if it shows up at all — is a hitchhiker we pick up along the way.

The results are predictable: disillusionment, heartbreak, or, in the worst cases, a marriage that should have remained a weekend fling.

With age, however, something shifts. Experience — that stern but effective teacher — leaves its marks. We become more cautious, more discerning, more aware of the emotional price tag attached to impulsive intimacy. The older we get, the more we realize that a long-term relationship requires more than chemistry. It requires character, compatibility, and the kind of friendship that can withstand the inevitable storms.

Of course, this assumes that a long-term relationship is the goal. If someone is still in "player mode," enjoying short-term encounters and avoiding commitment, then the calculus is different. But even the most dedicated players eventually reach a point where the thrill fades, and the desire for something lasting emerges. Biology may drive youth, but time has a way of humbling even the most ardent libertines.

Can upbringing, values, or religious teachings instill the discipline to delay gratification? Perhaps. Some youth groups attempt to revive celibacy-until-marriage traditions as a corrective to the post-sexual-revolution landscape. But most young people embrace the freedom of instant gratification. Trying to put an old head on young shoulders is an exercise in futility. They will learn the way we learned — through mistakes, heartbreak, and the occasional emotional hangover.

Meanwhile, those of us in the "venerable" category approach intimacy differently. We may fantasize about falling head over heels again — the intoxicating rush of early love — but most of us wake up from that dream quickly. We move slowly, cautiously, and deliberately. Without procreation as a priority, our needs shift. We want companionship, reliability, emotional safety, and a partner who feels like a best friend. The loins no longer dictate the pace; the heart and mind take over.

In the world of digital dating, this has become even more important. Some people sign up for a six-month membership and want to explore their options before committing. Others are ready to settle down after the first promising encounter. If you're in the exploratory phase, becoming intimate too soon can create expectations neither party is prepared to meet. For many, physical intimacy implies commitment — even if that wasn't the intention.

The antidote is honest communication. State your intentions early. Clarify what you want and what you don't. It may take several conversations before both people understand what the other truly offers. Transparency prevents misunderstandings and minimizes hurt.

By moving slowly — before sexual vulnerability clouds judgment — we give ourselves the chance to build something solid. This is the advice our elders gave us when we were young. We ignored it, had our fun, and paid the price. Eventually, after enough pain, we become willing to try a healthier approach.

Addendum: What fascinates me about mature dating is how many older adults remain "players," stuck in a time warp, trying to relive who they once were — or who they never had the chance to be. Certain medications add fuel to the illusion, creating a late-in-life super-stud fantasy. They rush in, exhilarated, rather than taking their time. Maybe a good marriage can still emerge from that approach, but it's a lower-percentage shot than building a foundation of friendship first. Ultimately, it depends on what one believes they have to offer. Some rely on sexual prowess; others know they bring more to the table — and move slowly.

REGRETTABLY OUT OF SYNC

"It well becomes a man who is no longer young to forget that he ever was." —
Seigneur de Saint-Evremond (1696)

Every once in a very rare while, someone appears who seems to
possess all the qualities we've spent a lifetime searching for — plus
that mysterious X factor that bypasses logic and goes straight to the
soul. It has happened to me so infrequently that I've spent years
single, unwilling to settle for anything less than the combination of
depth, resonance, and emotional chemistry that moves me to commit.

I sensed it early with her. Something in the way she scanned the room,
the cadence of her speech, the emotional intelligence behind her
words. She seemed open, vulnerable, honest — at least initially. I
asked her for dinner, fully aware that the age gap might make the
invitation unwelcome. But like many men of my vintage, I still
operate under the delusion that I'm youthful, energetic, and appealing.
So, I took the risk.

She accepted — with the clear stipulation that the evening would be
strictly platonic. I agreed, though I wanted more. And almost
immediately, I told her so. If romance was off the table, I would honor
that boundary and welcome her friendship.

But is such a friendship realistic? Or am I setting myself up for
heartbreak? Will she sense my deeper longing and withdraw to avoid
the inevitable disappointment? Am I relying on the old fantasy that
"given enough time, she'll fall in love," even though the
circumstances make that unlikely and perhaps unwise?

Beyond the intangible pull, she is impressive in every concrete way:
intelligent, compassionate, grounded, a physician with strong values
and a desire to become a mother as she approaches forty. Her life has
been devoted to building a career; now she wants to balance it with
family. That is natural — and incompatible with where I am in life.

Over the years, I've told many women I didn't want to have another child. But life has a way of mocking our certainties. As my mother used to say in Yiddish, *Mentsh planz un Got lacht* — man plans and God laughs.

Perhaps I balked in the past because I wasn't truly in love. Can one know from the outset? Many people claim they did — that they "just knew." I never believed them. I assumed it was limerence, that intoxicating blend of fantasy and infatuation that masquerades as destiny. A crush with a PhD.

And yet here I am, asking myself, "Jack, are you losing your mind?" Am I letting a romantic fantasy override reality? I barely know this woman. I don't know how she handles stress, what her quirks are, how she relates to others, what her touch feels like, her scent, her emotional rhythms — all the essential ingredients of real love. And still, something in me is stirring.

Pascal wrote, "Love has its reasons for which reason knows nothing." I seem to be living inside that paradox.

If nothing comes of this — if we remain friends briefly or not at all — I've learned something important: I am still capable of feeling. I thought I had aged out of limerence, that decades of psychiatric work and personal experience had stripped me of the ability to idealize anyone. Idealization is the fuel of early love, and I assumed that tank was empty.

Perhaps this is regression — a return to a younger self who could still be swept away by possibility. The ecstasy of imagining the "woman with the golden apples" is a high unlike any other. Why not savor it while it lasts? These moments are rare, and life is short.

Of course, she will eventually reveal her flaws, as all humans do. The question is whether they will be fatal or simply part of the package one accepts in a mature relationship.

I did notice something on our evening together: she was more interesting than interested. That could be a character flaw — or simply a sign that she didn't want to encourage closeness. Or perhaps it reflects the difference between a psychiatrist and a surgeon. My instinct is to ask questions; hers may be to avoid them.

When I finally asked if she had anything she wanted to know about me, she said "no" — plainly, without hesitation. No follow-up questions. No curiosity. Even friends usually want to know something. Perhaps "friendship" was lip service. Perhaps "next time" was a polite fiction. I hope not. I'd like to see whether we can sustain a genuine friendship without romantic overtones. Life teaches through experience, not theory.

For a fleeting moment, I felt young again — hopeful, vital, open to the possibility of falling in love. If not with her, then perhaps with someone like her, someone whose life goals are not so regrettably out of sync with mine. She arrived like an angel, offering a glimpse of what I still want and need. For that, I am grateful. I hope she finds the man who can give her what she seeks. I'd like to believe she wishes the same for me.

Addendum: Writing this essay helps me work through the vulnerability of being captivated by a young woman who, in the end, is unsuitable. In another era of my life, she would have been a delightful interlude. But those intervals have grown thin in the autumn of my years.

It is hard-wired in men to long for who we once were — the younger selves who effortlessly attracted younger women. But that fantasy is best left to the rich and famous. For most men, the younger woman's affection is tied to power, prestige, or financial security. And for the older man, the "love" he feels is often an illusion — a youth transfusion, an ego boost, not a sustainable bond.

With restraint and clarity, I see the truth: an age-appropriate woman is far more likely to be my true partner. The challenge now is to act on that insight. Time will tell whether I follow through — or whether I remain, as John Heywood warned, "an old fool."

CONFUSION AND DIMINISHED SEXUAL POWER

"Everything in the world is about sex except sex. Sex is about power." — Oscar Wilde.

From adolescence onward, most men find themselves oriented toward pursuing women. It feels less like a choice and more like a biological imperative — a hard-wired instinct that shapes our attention, our fantasies, and, for many, the architecture of our days. When we're not channeling that energy into sports, work, or distraction, our minds drift back to the feminine — to desire, longing, and the intoxicating pull of possibility.

As young men, testosterone fuels the chase. We roam dormitories, bars, parties, gyms — anywhere the promise of connection might flicker. Later, as adults, we migrate to happy hours, health clubs, dating apps, and every conceivable venue where attraction might spark. The pursuit becomes a kind of compass, orienting us toward meaning, excitement, and identity.

For many men, this dynamic becomes a form of sexual power — the sense of vitality, confidence, and purpose that comes from desire and the possibility of reciprocation. It is addictive, intoxicating, and deeply woven into the male psyche. And for a long time, it feels eternal.

But nothing in life is eternal.

At some point — gradually or abruptly — the intensity wanes. The once-overpowering drive softens, quiets, or disappears altogether. And then the question emerges: *Who am I without this?*

It's not an easy question. People will offer well-meaning suggestions — hobbies, travel, meditation, golf — but none of these fully replace the primal thrill of pursuit, the ego-affirming joy of being desired, or the emotional electricity of intimacy. For many men, sexuality has been a defining force, a source of identity, and a measure of vitality.

So where does the urge go? Age plays a role. Hormones decline. Energy shifts. The glittering allure of youthful sexuality loses some of its shine. The risks — emotional, physical, medical — become more salient. Sexually transmitted infections among older adults are on the rise, and caution tempers spontaneity.

Then there is the cultural shift: the "new woman," confident, assertive, and often comfortable initiating intimacy. For men accustomed to being the pursuer, this reversal can feel disorienting. Add to that the physical realities of aging — prostate surgery, diabetes, vascular issues, spinal injuries — and the male identity as "hunter" can feel compromised.

For some men, the transition is gradual and manageable. For others, it is sudden — the result of illness, surgery, or trauma — and the psychological impact can be profound. A loving, long-term relationship can buffer the blow, offering security and tenderness that transcend performance. But for single men, or those in strained marriages, the loss can feel like an existential crisis.

Medical interventions — from medications to implants — can help, but they rarely restore the effortless confidence of youth. Re-entering the dating world can feel like stepping into an arena where younger, more physically capable men dominate. The comparison is inevitable, and often painful.

Some men withdraw. Others fight fiercely to reclaim what they can. Ultimately, the healthiest adaptation is acceptance — not resignation, but a reorientation toward a different kind of intimacy.

Many women, especially later in life, value tenderness, affection, emotional presence, and sensuality far more than athletic performance. They do not require acrobatics or marathon endurance. They want a connection. They want warmth. They want to feel cherished. And they mean it — even when men doubt their sincerity.

Some women will walk away, seeking the vitality of a younger partner. But many will adapt, embracing what their partner *can* offer, and supplementing what he cannot with creativity, communication, and mutual understanding. Contrary to stereotype, most women do not derive pleasure from holding sexual power over a man. They want partnership, not dominance.

Addendum: If one has the patience to navigate this new landscape, it is entirely possible to find a woman who appreciates everything a man can offer — emotionally, intellectually, spiritually — regardless of physical limitations. Life has a way of providing what we need, though it may look very different from what we once imagined. And sometimes, the absence of the old sexual power creates space for a deeper, more authentic connection — one not built on pursuit or performance, but on presence, tenderness, and truth.

DUPLICITY

"We are so accustomed to disguising ourselves to others that in the end, we become disguised to ourselves." — François de La Rochefoucauld.

It takes a long time to know another human being truly. Some people are transparent — what you see is what you get. Others remain enigmatic, elusive, and impenetrable, no matter how much time you spend with them. And then there are those rare individuals who charm, disarm, and ultimately deceive, leaving you vulnerable in the hands of someone who has mastered the art of concealment.

It happens in novels and films all the time. But to admit it happened to me — a trained, seasoned psychiatrist — is a bitter pill to swallow. Yet it did.

The story began in February 2004. Note that certain descriptive parts that follow are intentionally repeated, from My ballerina. I was on the elliptical machine at my gym when I noticed a thin blonde woman beside me, reading *The New York Times* while exercising vigorously. Her posture, her carriage, her focus — everything suggested a dancer. I asked if she was a ballerina. Without hesitation, she said yes. She told me she had danced with the American Ballet Theatre. And then, as if I were back in my office, I asked if she was anorexic. She looked startled and asked if I was a psychiatrist. I said yes.

From that brief exchange, a relationship began — one that lasted, on and off, for more than twelve years. I once believed we loved each other. Today, I question whether that was ever possible. How can you love someone you never truly knew?

She told me she was thirty-four, divorced, childless, a former ABT dancer, a graduate of elite New York prep schools, and an Ivy League college. She claimed to be the sole surviving member of her family — her parents deceased, her only brother recently dead of a heart attack. She refused to let me attend the funeral. She never showed me photographs of her past — no family, no childhood, no ballet. Her apartments were stark, devoid of personal history. She said memories made her unbearably sad.

She lived as a minimalist, leasing expensive apartments and cars but owning nothing. She claimed to be the trustee of a large inheritance, managed by financial advisors. She spoke of famous dancers, artistic directors, and even a well-known political figure to whom she said she was related. Some of it seemed plausible. Much of it did not. But I suspended disbelief, sensing her fragility and wanting to protect her.

Over the years, others told me she had children with her former husband, a prominent physician. Each time I asked, she vehemently denied it. She insisted that the children were from his previous marriage. I wanted to believe her.

Fourteen months after we stopped speaking, I finally investigated. With the help of a friend, I found the truth: she had two grown children — a thirty-four-year-old physician and a twenty-five-year-old fitness entrepreneur. Her age was not thirty-four when we met, but closer to fifty. She had shaved sixteen years off her life and erased her own children.

Seeing their photographs, with her name and her former husband's name listed as parents, was devastating. Not just because she lied to me — but because I suddenly understood the magnitude of the life she had been hiding. The secrecy. The shame. The loneliness. The fear of being exposed.

Her brother's "funeral," her refusal to introduce me to friends or family, the absence of photographs — it all made sense. She had built a life behind a curtain, terrified that the truth would collapse the fragile identity she had constructed.

I felt betrayed, yes. But I also felt profound sadness for her. What must have happened to create such a need for reinvention? What pain, what humiliation, what trauma?

I considered calling her, confronting her, and asking why she lied. I wanted to understand. I wanted closure. But I also knew that contacting her might reopen wounds I had barely begun to heal.

Then, on my birthday, she called — as she had the year before. This time, she asked me to return the call. I did. And I read the entire essay I had written about her duplicity.

She interrupted repeatedly, insisting it was all untrue. She said she was forty-six, not sixty-two. She said the children were not hers — that she had acted as a surrogate mother figure, not a biological one. She said her former husband had manipulated documents, and that she would show me her birth certificate and driver's license to prove her age.

She told me she loved me, missed me, and had been too traumatized by her marriage to commit to me. She said she would explain everything — later.

And then, predictably, she retreated into ambiguity. Texts without clarity. Promises without follow-through. A return to the nebulous, enigmatic dance that had defined our relationship for more than a decade.

My heart reacted before my mind did. That night, for the first time in months, I felt the familiar flutter of arrhythmia — the same sensation that preceded my atrial fibrillation before my cardiac ablation. Perhaps it was a coincidence. Perhaps not. The body often knows before the mind does.

My unconscious was speaking clearly: let it go.

Self-preservation sometimes outweighs compassion. I spent years trying to rescue her from herself. I cannot do it anymore. She will have to save herself.

Addendum: There has been no further communication. As time passes, my need to know diminishes. I may never learn the full truth. Perhaps one day I will encounter someone who can fill in the missing pieces. Or perhaps the mystery will remain intact. Either way, I am learning to accept that some stories do not resolve neatly — and some people remain unknowable, even after twelve years.

CLOSING THE DEAL

"You always have two choices: your commitment versus your fear." — Sammy Davis Jr.

The other night, after a long and unexpectedly intimate conversation with a woman, I've been intermittently involved with for years, I found myself asking a question I've spent decades avoiding: *What would it take for me to finally close the deal?*

For most of my adult life, I've sidestepped remarriage with the agility of a seasoned escape artist. I've had no shortage of justifications — some rational, others cleverly disguised fear. The truth is that the prospect of another divorce feels like emotional and financial Armageddon. Even writing about it makes my pulse quicken. My internal ecology has been protecting me from an institution I distrust.

After typing that paragraph, I shut down my computer and went to sleep. That night, my unconscious staged a Broadway-level production. I dreamed I was wandering around a neighborhood resembling Georgetown, unable to find my car. Had it been stolen? Towed? Or had I simply forgotten where I parked? The relief I felt upon waking — knowing my car was safely in my garage — was enormous.

In the same dream, I found myself in a restaurant where people were gambling with small rolled-up pieces of dough used to make bread. One doesn't need Freud or Fellini to decode that metaphor. Losing the car — losing what is mine, losing my bearings, losing control — is a perfect stand-in for the fear of marriage. And the dough? Well, that symbolism practically explains itself.

The woman in question is a psychiatrist, recently divorced, mother of two grown daughters, living in Washington, D.C. She speaks of marriage with a kind of romantic idealism that feels both touching and impractical. She doesn't want a prenuptial agreement. I understand her longing for security — especially if she were to give up her practice and move in with me — but at this stage of life, a prenup is not optional. It's self-preservation.

I'm not entirely sure I want to spend the rest of my life with her. We haven't tested the daily realities of living together. I've done "test runs" with other women before, and they didn't lead to marriage — not exactly a glowing endorsement of the method. But I'm not the same man I was then, and she is exceptional in her own way. Timing matters.

I think about arranged marriages around the world — unions that "work" not because of compatibility but because of commitment. But what does "work" even mean? The criteria vary wildly across cultures, families, and personal histories. My own criteria may be too idealistic, too perfectionistic, too rooted in the fantasy of effortless harmony. The old adage *marriage takes work* has never appealed to me. Give me a grounded, emotionally evolved partner, and the relationship should run smoothly. Perhaps that's another fantasy.

We've spent vacations together, long weekends, and countless conversations. The emotional intimacy is often lovely — the oxytocin-infused cuddling, the affectionate banter, the shared humor. But her reluctance to engage in passionate sexual intimacy gives me pause. I joked that if she waited long enough, my testosterone would drop and the issue would resolve itself. Humor aside, I need that connection. Without it, we risk becoming housemates — a prelude to irritability and breakdown.

She cites fear of sexually transmitted diseases. I've reassured her repeatedly — my bloodwork is pristine — but I suspect something deeper is at play. Her previous marriage lacked intimacy. She says she enjoyed sex with another man, but was that genuine pleasure or accommodation? She doesn't say. She rarely volunteers anything about her inner world.

She is a triathlete, exercises obsessively, and has minimal body fat. Perhaps her hormonal levels are altered. Perhaps she is post-menopausal. Perhaps she is simply not driven sexually. I've even wondered — fleetingly — whether she might be gay. Everything is on the table when communication is limited.

At times, she feels withholding, parsimonious with emotional disclosure. The fourth of five children, perhaps more accustomed to being cared for than caring. At other times, I wonder if she simply doesn't know how to be emotionally intimate. She avoids therapy, claiming she doesn't need it. As a psychiatrist, I find that both ironic and concerning. Her early training as a surgeon and radiologist may have reinforced a more concrete, left-brained style — the opposite of the intuitive, emotionally attuned psychiatrist she later became.

Our first sexual encounter occurred shortly after my radical prostatectomy in 2003 — a difficult moment for me, one that may have set a psychological precedent. Later, with another woman who had patience and desire, I healed. But with this woman, I received no encouragement, no sensual reciprocity, no passion. My confidence faltered. I became reactive and frustrated. She may have given up on me sexually just as I was struggling to regain my footing.

She is twenty-one years younger. She worries about losing me to age. I told her that, unless I inherit my mother's longevity — she lived to 101 — her fear is realistic. But her mother is in her nineties and thriving. Longevity is a wild card.

We both have reasons to hesitate. And yet, she is in many ways the most comfortable choice. We have history. We have affection. We have compatibility in many domains. But how much compromise is too much? At what point does adaptation become self-betrayal?

Another painful possibility: perhaps she does not trust or love me enough to surrender sexually. She admits she fears my occasional emotional confrontations. Love and fear cannot coexist. If we can resolve this, perhaps everything else will fall into place.

She says she will retire and travel with me. She says she could give up her practice tomorrow. She is social, multilingual, adaptable, intelligent, and kind. She gets along with my daughter; I get along with her's. On paper, she meets many criteria.

It would be the right thing to do — enthusiastically, decisively — for what is likely the last time in my life. Going solo has its pleasures, but too much solitude becomes stale. I feel ready for a major shift. But readiness alone is not enough. I must listen to my dream, to my unconscious, to the wisdom beneath the fear.

Perhaps she is not the woman for me. Or perhaps this is what mature love feels like — less fireworks, more quiet resonance.

Addendum: People rarely change without a seismic life event or deep therapeutic work. What we see may be all there is, and that might be enough. Or it might not. There may be a vast reservoir beneath her surface, but it is not my job to excavate it. If we can accept each other respectfully and unconditionally, perhaps everything will unfold smoothly. Or perhaps that is another pipe dream. As the Buddhists say, we'll see.

MY MOTHER APPROACHES 100

"There is only one difference between a long life and a good dinner: that, in the dinner, the sweets come last." — Robert Louis Stevenson.

My mother is approaching 100. It's only a number, yes — but a number so few reach that it demands reflection. I once asked her for the secret to her longevity. She paused, shrugged, and said, "I have no clue; it's a great mystery." Then, in her trademark quasi-philosophical style, she added, "You've got to do everything in moderation. Nothing to extremes." And in Yiddish, the addendum: *Tsu fil es ungezunt* — too much of anything is unhealthy.

I've always marveled at her ability to produce instant wisdom, as if she had a private hotline to the universe. Was it genuine insight? Or a survival mechanism — a way of imposing order on a life that had often been chaotic and painful? I suspect the latter. She never questioned her own pronouncements; doubt would have undone her. Certainty was her armor.

The truth is, no one knows why someone lives to 100. The simplest explanation is that she didn't die. Add a state-of-the-art pacemaker and a constitution forged in hardship, and the rest is speculation.

She was born in 1909 in Siauliai, Lithuania, the fifth of eight children. All her siblings are gone; she is the last of her generation. She came to Canada in 1928 with two brothers, joining older siblings near Montreal. Her parents stayed behind to settle financial matters, intending to follow. They never made it. The Nazis murdered them in a concentration camp. Two younger siblings survived and eventually reached Canada.

She carried that loss her entire life. In 1945, her uncles came to New York to tell her the news. She was devastated. If stress truly shortened lives, she would have died decades ago. Instead, she endured.

She divorced my father when I was young, raised me alone during World War II, remarried briefly, divorced again, and sent me to boarding school from second to fifth grade so she could work and keep me in private school. It was a mixed experience, but probably the best she could do.

She had a seven-year relationship while I was away, then moved us to Florida in 1953. I worked to help support us — a heavy burden for a boy, and one I suspect filled her with guilt. She remarried when I was sixteen, and for the first time, I could save money for college and medical school.

Her husband died suddenly in 1976, leaving her with nothing. I stepped in again. And for the next thirty-three years, I became her caretaker — emotionally, financially, logistically. She has no one else. My daughter calls and visits, but the day-to-day responsibility is mine.

I escort her to doctors, shop for her, manage her bills, and handle her affairs. I avoid long trips because her medical crises always seem to occur when I'm away. She never had the temperament or skills to manage these things herself. She relied on her husbands, and when they passed, she relied on me.

And here's the truth: it isn't conflict-free. The Hallmark version — the grateful son giving back to the mother who gave him everything — is not my story. She loved me, yes. But she also criticized, worried, scolded, and justified it all by saying, "If I didn't care, I wouldn't get so angry." As a child, I believed her. As an adult, I know better. A little compassion would have gone a long way.

Now she is frail, hard of hearing, often falls, blames me for speaking too softly, and forgets instructions about her walker. I find myself snapping back at her — a reflexive echo of her own invectives from my childhood. I'm not proud of it. Sometimes I catch myself, soften, and feel the sadness of watching her decline. Lately, I've been more patient, more attuned to the reality that time is running out.

She often says she's had enough and doesn't understand why she hasn't died yet. I understand. At 100, life is more burden than a blessing. I told her she had to stay alive until her birthday so my daughter and I could claim bragging rights. She laughed and said, "Okay, I'll stick around a little longer. After that, all bets are off."

I ask if she fears death. "Not at all," she says. I envy that. At seventy, I feel more like Woody Allen: I'm not afraid of dying — I just don't want to be there when it happens.

Perhaps nature prepares us for death when we reach extreme old age. When nearly everyone you've loved is gone, when your body betrays you daily, when life becomes a series of small indignities, the desire to let go makes sense.

Sometimes I sit with her for hours — lunch, laundry, conversation, or silence. She seems content. She has adapted to her solitude. The television, the phone, the occasional visitor — it seems enough. She doesn't complain. She smiles and says she's fine. And maybe she is.

When I imagine her gone, I feel the sadness rising. I will miss her constancy — her reliability, her dependability, her presence. I will miss her answering the phone, listening, talking, and even criticizing. I will miss her philosophical musing, even if they were more about maintaining control than dispensing truth.

Addendum: My mother gave me everything she could, within the limits of who she was. She was imperfect, flawed, wounded — and loving in her own way. I love her deeply. And when she leaves this earth, I will miss her more than I can say.

MY MOTHER'S PROTECTOR

"To a mother, a son is never a fully grown man; and a son is never a fully grown man until he understands and accepts this about his mother." — Author Unknown.

It is self-evident that a parent will do whatever it takes to protect a child. The question — the one that becomes more urgent as our parents age — is whether a child will do the same for a parent. And if so, at what emotional cost?

My mother is now six months past her 100th birthday. Frail, exhausted, and showing unmistakable signs of heart failure, she often wonders aloud why she is still alive. As a retired physician, I monitor her closely. When her lungs fill with fluid, and her legs swell, I urge her to take diuretics to prevent the terrifying sensation of drowning — a death I hope she never experiences. I want her to slip away peacefully, in her sleep, without fear or struggle.

She is ready to go. I've told her how much I love her and how deeply I will miss her. She tells me I've been lucky to have a mother for over seventy years. Sometimes she refuses her medication, trying to hasten the end. I coax her back, reminding her that breathing easily is worth fighting for. Each time, she is relieved to feel her lungs open again.

She still cooks, manages most of her daily needs, and insists on her independence. After a pelvic fracture, she began using a four-wheeled walker with hand brakes and a seat — a contraption that allows me to push her when her stamina fails.

A few days ago, I took her to Mt. Sinai Hospital for a pacemaker check. As soon as she stepped out of the car, she ran out of breath and had to sit. I placed her on the walker and began pushing her toward the hospital entrance.

Then it happened.

The wheels caught on a defect in the pavement. The walker jerked. My mother began to fall backward toward the cement. Instinct took over. I lunged to catch her, breaking her fall — but with my hands occupied, I had no way to protect myself. I slammed face-first into the concrete.

The impact was brutal. Blood poured from my nose. For a moment, I thought I had shattered my face. I looked over at my mother — motionless — and feared the worst. Then she opened her eyes.

I apologized through the blood. People stared, horrified. Someone ran for help. Another helped me lift her back onto the walker. I wheeled her down the hallway, blood dripping onto my clothes, my adrenaline carrying me forward.

In the cardiology office, the nurse handed me gauze. I cleaned myself up enough to function. My mother was taken in for her pacemaker check. I discovered a deep gash on my nose, but no fracture. I had dodged a bullet.

The image of her falling backward haunts me. The sensation of my face hitting the cement replays in my mind. Sleep has been difficult. It is, without question, a form of post-traumatic stress.

Later, as I wheeled her to her cardiologist, she began blaming me — insisting she could have walked on her own. She had forgotten that she could barely take a few steps before collapsing. She had no awareness of how close she came to a catastrophic head injury. Do I want acknowledgment? It would be nice. But I can live without it. What I cannot live with is blame.

I have been my mother's protector for most of my life — emotionally, financially, and physically. She refuses assisted living. She values her independence. I respect that. I would like the same. When I hired help, she begged me to let the caregiver go. So, I did.

She survived the fall with only a sore back. My nose will heal. Her heart failure continues to respond to treatment. But the psychological impact lingers.

Had she died, I would have blamed myself — irrationally, but inevitably. I would have blamed the hospital for the defective pavement. I would have replayed the moment endlessly. The attorneys might have had a case, but what jury would be moved by the death of a frail centenarian or the injuries of a son who had her for seventy years?

Some in my profession — including the part of me trained to think psychoanalytically — might suggest unconscious motives: a death wish toward my mother, followed by guilt and a heroic rescue. But sometimes a fall is just a fall. As Freud said, "Sometimes a cigar is just a cigar." Not every accident is a psychological Rorschach.

Her death — whenever it comes — will devastate me. I want her to go peacefully, not violently. And I want to know, on some level, that she understood how much I tried to protect her.

My mother has never been one to express gratitude. She has rarely apologized. She has never said "I love you" or hugged me. She believes words are meaningless; only actions count. She is partly right — but also partly wrong. Words matter. They soothe. They repair. They connect.

She taught me integrity, dependability, reliability, and constancy. But she also taught me criticism, anger, and emotional distance. As a child, I could not reconcile her tirades with love. I concluded she didn't love me — or that I was unlovable. That conclusion shaped my relationships for decades.

Only recently have I come to understand that love and anger can coexist. That a mother can love deeply and still be flawed, reactive, and overwhelmed. That my childhood interpretation was just that — a child's interpretation.

A few months ago, while filming our annual Thanksgiving video, I asked her — one last time — if she loved me. She looked at me, gathered what strength she had left, and said, "What else could it be? You've been my life. Look at me — how I've been there for you the way you are for me."

I cried. I felt her love. I felt her acknowledgment. I felt her gratitude. An apology was no longer necessary.

Addendum: It has taken me a lifetime to understand my mother — to forgive her limitations, to see her love beneath the criticism, to accept her humanity. Many never reach this point. I am grateful I did, even if it came late. We never truly know what another person feels. We interpret, infer, and construct meaning. My peace depends on believing that she loved me in the only way she could — imperfectly, fiercely, and consistently. My task now is simple: to protect her until she takes her leave.

GOING GENTLY INTO THE NIGHT

"To die proudly when it is no longer possible to live proudly… death at the proper time, with a clear head and with joyfulness… so that an actual leave-taking is possible while he who is leaving is still there." — Friedrich Nietzsche.

Dying can be merciless — a slow, painful unraveling that tests the endurance of everyone involved. But every so often, life grants a rare mercy: a gentle exit, free of suffering, where the final moments unfold with clarity, tenderness, and grace. My mother was given that gift.

She nearly reached 101. A few more months and she would have crossed that symbolic threshold, but the truth is, longevity had long since lost its meaning. Her life had become a fragile balancing act between independence and exhaustion. Her mind remained sharp, but her body had reached its limit. She was still cooking, still insisting on doing things "her way," until the final week, when she fell several times. Nothing broke — a small miracle — but she no longer had the strength to lift herself. Emergency services had to come each time.

Her heart was failing. Aortic insufficiency had finally claimed its due. Fluid backed up into her lungs; her legs swelled. The thought of her drowning in her own fluids was unbearable. I increased her Lasix to twice a day. It helped, but only briefly. And the price was steep: she spent the nights awake, urinating endlessly, exhausted and sleep-deprived.

For the next week, she slept for hours at a time — something utterly foreign to her. That was when I brought in 24-hour hospice care. She met the criteria for end-stage congestive heart failure and failure to thrive.

Until then, she had fiercely resisted the idea of a caretaker. Independence was her last remaining dignity. I admired that. I would like the same. But this time, she accepted the nurses, reluctantly but without protest. Her breathing grew erratic. She slept more. She struggled to move air into her lungs. I looked at the nurse and said quietly, "I think she's getting close. I've never seen her like this."

When she woke, she called me over. I sat beside her. In a moment of absolute lucidity — the kind that feels like a final clearing of the clouds — she said:

"Jack, I feel this is the end. I can feel it coming… in my heart. I have little time left and want to tell you that you have been the greatest son a mother could want. I love you. Thank you. I want you to know how grateful I am for all you have given me."

Her words pierced me. I broke down. I hugged her, kissed her, and cried on her shoulder. When I could speak again, I said:

"Mom, I am so thankful to have had you for 71 years. You have been a blessing and a gift. You gave me life and devotion. You were always there for me. I love you, and I will miss you more than I can say."

She squeezed my hand. Then she said, "Call Lisa. I want to talk to her."

I called my daughter. My mother told her how much she loved her, how grateful she was for their years together, how much she would miss her. I watched her smile as she listened to Lisa's voice for the last time. The nurse stood nearby, crying.

Afterward, I thought she might rest better in an inpatient hospice setting. She hadn't slept for days. But the double room she was placed in — shared with a woman clearly at death's door — terrified her. When I arrived the next morning, she begged me to take her home. She wanted to die in her own bed.

I asked the nurse to move her to a private room and give her a small dose of lorazepam. After the medication, she softened. She smiled again. I tucked her into the fresh linens, dimmed the lights, and sat with her in the quiet, peaceful room.

"Mom," I said, "get a good night's sleep. I'll see you in the morning."

"Yes," she whispered, "a very long, good sleep."

"Take as long as you want."

She opened her eyes one last time. With the last of her strength, she said:

"Jack, promise me you will find a good woman to take care of you."

I held her hand and said, "Yes, Mom. I promise."

She smiled. Then she drifted off.

Several hours later, she died.

My heart is heavy. She lived almost 101 years — not an easy life, but one devoted to her son and granddaughter. She died exactly as she wished: peacefully, in her sleep, without pain, without tubes or machines, without strangers hovering over her. She said what she needed to say. My daughter and I said what we needed to say. Permission was given. Love was exchanged. And she went gently into that night.

Addendum: There are moments in life when everything aligns — timing, clarity, presence, love — and the ending becomes not just bearable, but beautiful. My mother's death was one of those rare moments. A perfect leave-taking. A final gift.

MOTHER'S DEATH — A GIANT VOID

"A mother is the truest friend we have… when trouble thickens around us, still will she cling to us, and endeavor by her kind precepts and counsels to dissipate the clouds of darkness and cause peace to return to our hearts." — Washington Irving.

My mother's death has created a breach in my life so vast that I am still learning how to walk around it. For decades, my days were shaped — consciously and unconsciously — around her needs, her rhythms, her fragility, her presence. Now, several weeks after her passing, I find myself in a strange, disorienting state, as if the scaffolding that held my emotional world in place has quietly vanished.

She lived for nearly 101 years. For most of my life, I was her emotional and financial caretaker. Except for the brief periods when she was married or had a companion, I was the one who watched over her. When she became a widow in 1976, I stepped back into the role without hesitation. In the early years, it wasn't difficult — more a steady hum of responsibility than a burden. But the awareness was always there: *Make sure she's safe. Make sure she's okay.*

I loved my mother deeply. It was just the two of us for as long as I can remember. No extended family, no siblings, no safety net — only her and me. To have had her for seventy-one years is a blessing, but it also means I never knew adult life without her. Her absence now feels surreal, as if a foundational pillar has been quietly removed.

She lived alone, socializing occasionally, but spent most of her time by herself in her late nineties. I checked in several times a day — visits, phone calls, small conversations that anchored us both. She was always home. Always reachable. Always there. A constant presence, a reliable voice, a source of wisdom delivered with urgency, as if she knew time was running short and wanted to finish her life's work as a mother.

And while she was alive, she provided something intangible yet powerful: an illusory sense of protection. Even at 100, she could absorb my fears the way a parent absorbs a child's — not through action, but through presence. Her optimism, her stubborn belief that things would work out, acted as a buffer against my own darker assumptions. Now the buffer is gone. I face the uncertainties of aging and illness without her voice to soften the blow.

With the administrative tasks of her death now complete, the reality of her absence has settled in. I no longer begin my mornings by calling her. I no longer run to the store to restock her refrigerator or escort her to medical appointments, translating the doctor's words into something she could hear. I no longer stop by after golf to sit with her, fold her laundry, or simply share a quiet moment while the TV blared too loudly in the background. Those rituals — the small, ordinary acts of love — are gone.

In their place is a vast expanse of time. A giant void. I know I will fill it eventually, but the habits of decades do not dissolve overnight. My nervous system still expects to check on her. My mind still rehearses the old routines. It will take time to reprogram myself.

Evenings are the hardest. Without distractions, I feel her absence most acutely. I notice myself adopting her habits — the way I chew, the way my face moves, the way I clean or cook. Perhaps it is an unconscious defense against loss, a way of keeping her alive by becoming more like her. And when I use the food or household items I brought home from her apartment, I feel a pang of sadness as they run out. Soon, there will be nothing left that was hers. And I cry, because she is gone and not returning.

Her presence feels larger now than it was when she was alive.

I have no idea how this grieving process will unfold. I am in uncharted territory. This is my first time losing the person who shaped my entire life.

It is hurricane season. For years, every storm warning meant planning her evacuation from Miami Beach. My concern for her safety always outweighed my own. Now, for the first time, I only have to worry about myself. The absence of that responsibility feels both liberating and unsettling.

My vacations are now open-ended. No more rushing home from overseas because she needed me. No more calculating how far I could travel without risking being unreachable. Freedom has arrived — but it arrived through loss.

And yet, alongside the void, there is a gift: the lifting of a lifelong burden. I can now imagine taking the trips I postponed — China, India, and New Zealand. I can imagine living without the constant hum of vigilance. I can imagine joy without guilt.

I believe I took excellent care of her. I feel no remorse, no lingering doubt about what I did or didn't do. I received emotional remuneration for my efforts — her love, her gratitude, her final words.

Addendum: Learning to accept the adage that "life happens while you're making other plans" is not easy. But I will set my sails and hope the winds are kind. I will hone my skills and chart a new course. And if spirits or angels are watching over us — as I sometimes allow myself to believe — then my mother will be among them, endlessly present, whispering her love and wisdom into my mind, just as she did in life.

FAREWELL TO A GOOD FRIEND

" 'Tis better to buy a small bouquet And give your friend this very day, Than a bushel of roses, white and red, To lie on his coffin after he's dead." — Author Unknown.

Dear Barry,

I want you to know how honored I am to have had you as my closest friend for the past fifty-two years. While so many long-term friendships fade or drift apart, ours only deepened. We became brothers — loyal, devoted, and woven into each other's lives in ways that time could never erode.

As you prepare to leave this earth, I don't want to wait for a funeral to say what matters. I want you to hear it now, while you're still here, still you. Our friendship has been a tapestry of joy, mischief, laughter, and shared history — the kind of bond that becomes part of one's identity.

It began in 1958. You transferred to the University of Florida, and during rush week, I got you a bid and became your fraternity big brother. We clicked immediately. On the night of our graduation, we celebrated with a party that became legendary — complete with the divorced neighbor, her unexpected hospitality, and the unforgettable moment when her child walked in mid-charade. That story will outlive both of us.

After graduation, I stayed with your family in Brooklyn. They bumped Sister Wendy out of her bed so I could share your room. We cruised around in your father's Cadillac, feeling ultrahip in the West Village and Basin Street. You were the best-dressed man at UF, and you always let this poor kid borrow your stylish shirts from Neil's on King's Highway.

You became an attorney; I became a physician. We lived in different cities, but the friendship never wavered. When I returned to New

York for residency, we picked up right where we left off — mambo clubs, parties, and our famous kitchen-pot percussion routines. Two makeshift congueros, banging out rhythms that somehow entertained entire rooms. And the jokes — my God, the jokes. The Club Med marathon, where we had the whole dining room in stitches. You were the undisputed king of scatological humor, the two flies on the turd being your pièce de résistance.

You were a bachelor; I was divorced. We skied together in Aspen, Vail, Crested Butte, Snowbird — shushing down mountains with the vitality of young men and, later, the stubbornness of older ones. You dragged me into running, handed me a T-shirt and a number, and told me I was doing a 10K in Central Park. Eventually, we ran marathons together. I'll never forget the one in Washington where you stayed with me the entire race, even though you could have surged ahead. Friendship meant more to you than finishing time.

You were the consummate New Yorker — always up to date on the latest happenings. You took me to BAM, to off-Broadway plays in rooms the size of your living room, and to restaurants and events I never would have found on my own.

We played tennis, though your body held up longer than mine. Same with skiing — my neck, back, and knees eventually surrendered, but you kept going through moguls and powder until 2009. And then there was golf — the game neither of us could master, but both of us loved it. You were generous enough to bring me as your guest to St. Andrews and South Fork Country Clubs. I can never thank you enough.

I remember the Hamptons in the sixties — Martell's, Stephen Talkhouse, our attempts at picking up women, and that lunatic ex-marine landlord in Amagansett who nearly had me sleeping in my Porsche for driving a few miles over the limit.

You flew down for my 50th and 60th birthdays. We spent countless weekends together in New York. You even offered to sell me a one-bedroom in a Brownstone walk-up for $25,000 — and like a fool, I passed. You were right. I should have listened.

I knew all your girlfriends; you knew mine. Then came Jan, and then Ben — and your life blossomed. I came to your wedding and Ben's Bar Mitzvah. Watching him grow into a bright, athletic, extraordinary young man has been one of the joys of knowing you. You and Jan raised him beautifully.

You didn't make it to his high-school graduation. That was when the illness began its cruel unveiling. It breaks my heart to see you suffer. Life is fragile — one day everything is fine, and the next, everything changes. You are going where we are all going — some sooner, some later. And if there is something beyond this life, I hope we'll meet again on a golf course with perfect greens and no three-putts.

I will miss you terribly, my dear friend. You have been a gift — one I will cherish for the rest of my life. I'm grateful I got to see you recently. I wish I lived in New York so I could be with you every day, but having just buried my mother last week, circumstances made that impossible. So, I'm writing this letter for Jan to read to you — a bouquet given while you're still here to receive it.

Love you, brother, Jack

Addendum: Being an only child, I created my own siblings — friends who became family. Barry was the finest of them. A brother in every way that matters. I am grateful I had the chance to tell him what he meant to me before he left this world. It is a gift I recommend to anyone about to lose someone they love.

DEATH AND ITS IMPACT

"The life of the dead is placed in the memory of the living." — Marcus Tullius Cicero.

Death has a way of rearranging the psyche. It doesn't knock; it simply enters, sits down, and changes the atmosphere of a life. Today is sweltering and humid — the kind of day that invites staying indoors with the air-conditioning humming, trying to figure out how to structure the free time that has suddenly opened up. Perhaps it feels freer because my mother died a few weeks ago. And then, almost immediately, a dear friend of more than fifty years died an agonizing, unnatural death.

Losses like these place us in a strange, altered state — part grief, part numbness, part administrative competence. We handle the tasks required of a son or a friend, all while something inside us collapses. Only later, when the paperwork is done and the phone calls cease, do we begin to decompress, to feel, to grieve, to confront the void left behind.

The world continues, as it must. Friends and acquaintances move through their own daily stresses. Some have time to listen, to empathize, to share a moment of understanding. But for the most part, we drift back into solitude, sitting quietly in our homes, thinking, feeling, wondering what we must do with the time we have left before we, too, reach the end of the checkout line.

This has been a year of loss — all within the first six months of 2010.

First, Dr. Milton Berger died at ninety-one. A pioneer in his field, a mentor during my psychiatric residency at Columbia Presbyterian, and later a friend whose home in Montauk became a summer refuge for me since 1968.

Then came the death of my colleague and co-resident, Dr. Stanley Greenspan — perhaps the most well-known developmental child psychoanalyst in the world. Books, papers, television appearances — and now gone at sixty-nine.

Then my mother — my constant presence for nearly seventy-one years — died peacefully just short of 101.

And now Barry, my friend since 1957. A successful attorney, a great athlete, never sick a day in his life — until a ravaging illness took him within three months, leaving behind a wife and an eighteen-year-old son. The shock of it still reverberates.

It is said that as we age, our world shrinks unless we buffer it with children and grandchildren. That wasn't my path. My friends are my family, along with my daughter, Lisa.

Last week in New York, I sat on a bench overlooking the East River with my oldest friend from kindergarten, Freddie Horn. I still call him Freddie; he still calls me Jackie. If he were to leave this earth, I would be devastated. We promised each other we'd keep talking into our nineties — conversations likely filled with mutual aches and pains, but also with memories only we can validate for each other. There is something profoundly comforting about having someone who remembers your childhood, your youth, your foolishness, your triumphs — someone who can confirm that your life actually happened.

How many true friends can one have? A handful, if you're lucky. Bill Kaufman, another exceptional friend, is off hiking in Alaska. He has an aura of invincibility — seventy-one years of perfect health. If he were blindsided the way Barry was, I would feel even more unmoored, as if floating in a world of acquaintances rather than anchors. It reminds me of traveling alone in Europe for a month — after a few weeks, I would have to jump to London or Paris to see a friend, unable to tolerate the disconnection any longer.

Death — and the disconnection it leaves behind — has a way of clarifying what matters. It intensifies the longing for a lifetime partner. I have avoided that path for years, but now I feel the undercurrents of that choice.

It is time to move toward a true companion — someone who wants to be with me as much as I want to be with her. No games, no evasions, no emotional dodgeball. Someone capable of loving, honoring, and trusting. Someone who wants to sit beside me even when we do nothing at all, simply because being near each other feels right.

Once those essentials are present, the rest becomes irrelevant. We can travel the world or stay home. We can talk or sit in silence. What matters is the buffer we provide each other against the loneliness of bereavement and the inevitability of mortality.

Doing it alone feels increasingly untenable. Life has a way of teaching us what we need to know. Independence works for a while, but eventually the harsh jolts of experience remind us of the necessity of a loving, mutually dependent partnership.

Addendum: Finding that special person will still end in loss — nothing lasts forever. But given the alternative, in a life full of departures, we need a loving buffer, a place for the heart to rest, to be held, to find solace that cannot be found alone.

A NEW STATE OF MIND

"And I have seen the eternal Footman hold my coat, and snicker, And in short, I was afraid. I have seen the moment of my greatness flicker." — T. S. Eliot, *The Love Song of J. Alfred Prufrock.*

What I'm beginning to understand — slowly, reluctantly, but unmistakably — is that this new state of mind is not a detour. It's a threshold. Something in me is reorganizing after the double blow of losing my mother and losing a friend who had been woven into the fabric of my life for half a century. These losses have stripped away the illusion that time is abundant, that companionship can be postponed, that vulnerability is optional.

It isn't. Vulnerability is the price of admission for being alive.

And so, I sit here, in this beautiful home overlooking the ocean, feeling both the ache of solitude and the faint stirrings of possibility. It's a strange duality — the emptiness and the opening. The grief and the invitation. The loneliness and the quiet promise that something new might emerge if I allow myself to stay present long enough to feel it.

There is a subtle shift happening inside me. I can sense it in the way I look at the late-afternoon light on the water, in the way I linger over memories without collapsing into them, in the way I'm beginning to imagine a future that includes someone beside me — not as a fantasy, not as a placeholder, but as a genuine partner.

For the first time in a long time, I'm not trying to outrun my loneliness. I'm listening to it.

Loneliness, when you stop fighting it, becomes a teacher. It tells you what you truly need, not what you used to chase. It strips away the superficial, the performative, the ego-driven pursuits of youth. It leaves behind the essentials: connection, understanding, reciprocity, tenderness, and integrity.

I'm realizing that the next woman in my life — if she appears — will not be someone I charm or pursue with the old tools of seduction. She will be someone who meets me where I am now: a man who has lived, lost, learned, and is finally ready to be known without pretense.

Someone who can sit with me in silence without needing to fill it. Someone who can hear the tremor beneath my words. Someone who can offer comfort without criticism. Someone who understands that love at this stage of life is less about fireworks and more about presence.

This is not a resignation. It's clarity.

And clarity, I'm discovering, is its own form of peace.

I don't know when she will appear, or how, or in what form. I don't know whether she will arrive as a surprise or as a slow unfolding. But I do know this: I have cleared the emotional space for her. I have done the pruning, the grieving, the reckoning. I have faced the ghosts and the echoes. I have sat with the emptiness long enough to recognize it not as a punishment, but as preparation.

In the meantime, I will continue to live my life — golf, the gym, the small rituals that keep the body moving and the mind from stagnating. I will keep writing, because writing is the one place where I never feel alone. I will keep listening to the quiet, because the quiet is where the truth lives.

And I will keep my heart open — cautiously, yes, but open nonetheless — because the alternative is a slow emotional death, and I am not ready for that.

Not yet.

Addendum: Perhaps this is what maturity looks like: not the absence of longing, but the willingness to sit with it. Not the elimination of vulnerability, but the acceptance of it as a companion. And maybe —

just maybe — the next chapter of my life will not be defined by who I've lost, but by who I am finally ready to let in.

VULNERABLE BREAKTHROUGH

"When we were children, we used to think that when we were grown-up, we would no longer be vulnerable. But to grow up is to accept vulnerability... To be alive is to be vulnerable." — Madeleine L'Engle.

It began with the body's sudden collapse — a violent, humbling revolt after a simple meal gone wrong. Within hours, I was reduced to a trembling, feverish state: nausea in relentless waves, vomiting, chills, fainting, and a fatigue so complete it felt as if gravity had doubled. Illness has a way of stripping away the illusions of adulthood. In those moments, living alone feels like a verdict. I found myself wondering, again, why I am not sharing my life with someone who could steady me through these fragile hours.

And then, as she has done so many times before, my angelic ballerina appeared — not in person, but in presence. She has always been capable of rising to the moment when the stakes are high, even though her own life is constricted by the vise of an eating disorder. She is soft, kind, and instinctively nurturing. She was there during my episodes of atrial fibrillation, sitting with me all night in the emergency room, even curling up beside me on the narrow hospital bed as I waited for my heart to find its rhythm again. In those moments, she became "the good mother," the one who arrives when the world tilts.

This time, she did it again — but with a gesture that pierced me. She went to Epicure and gathered matzo ball soup, chicken in the pot, pumpernickel bread, fresh fruit, a cookie, and a copy of *The New York Times*. These were the maternal anchors of my childhood, except that back then, my mother substituted comic books — *Captain Marvel*, *Superman* — for the newspaper.

When the shopping bag appeared at my lobby desk, I dragged myself from bed, retrieved it, and returned upstairs. I opened the bag, read her handwritten note, and something inside me gave way. I sobbed — not a few tears, but a full, shaking, uncontrollable sob that lasted ten minutes or more. It was as if a long, sealed door had swung open.

Later, on the phone with her, I found myself drifting into memories — how her gesture echoed my mother, gone now a year, and how vividly I remembered being nurtured in this same way as a child. And then the double loss hit me: my mother gone, and my ballerina — who carries so much guilt about her inability to give me the sustained love I long for — preparing once again to retreat so as not to burden me with her unavailability.

It felt like too much. I told her I loved her, that I didn't want to lose her, that I understood her impulse to spare me pain by stepping away. It was a perfect catch-22: if she stayed, my heart ached; if she left, my heart shattered. Perhaps the only path is acceptance — that some love remains incomplete, and we must move forward anyway.

But the sobbing itself — the raw, cathartic release — felt strangely good. It had been years since I last cried like that. The previous time was after my prostate cancer diagnosis, lying on the couch in my mother's apartment as she cradled my face in her hands. She was not a woman given to touch or tenderness. Her instinct was usually to interrogate the cause, to assign blame, to insist that if only I had listened to her — taken fewer vitamins, exercised less, avoided stress — none of it would have happened. But that day, she said nothing. She simply held me. It was as if, for a moment, the preverbal mother returned — the one who soothed without judgment.

There have been other moments like this. Once, driving a borrowed car with my significant other, I hit a median strip on a dark, unfamiliar road. The damage was bad enough to require towing. I felt ashamed, shaken, out of control. She offered no criticism — only a quiet, steady presence. I sobbed again, and she simply stayed with me.

And then there was the boat — *Balmy Days*, the crossing from Boothbay Harbor to Monhegan Island. The sea was brutal. Within thirty minutes, nearly everyone except the crew and my girlfriend was vomiting. I was humiliated by my helplessness, this older psychiatrist, undone by the sea, while she, raised on Connecticut waters, remained unbothered. She held me, wiped my brow, stayed with me through every heave.

When we finally reached the island, I bolted off the boat and climbed to the top of its rocky spine. She followed. From the summit, I could see the island encircled by pounding waves, standing firm against the ocean's assault — the very unyieldingness I longed for in myself. She touched my hand lightly, and it felt like she touched my heart. I dropped to my knees and sobbed again — the kind of sob that empties you. She wrapped her arms around me and rocked me gently. Her silence was its own kind of sanctuary.

These are the episodes I remember. I'm sure infancy held countless others — helplessness is the native language of early life, and soothing is its grammar. If I had to wager, the intensity of these adult sobs is braided from those early maternal comforts and the later critical rebukes that overshadowed them. My tears are tears of loss — of longing for comfort rather than correction, for presence rather than admonishment. They remind me that some needs never outgrow us, especially when life delivers its unpredictable bolts from the blue. They remind me, too, of the necessity of a loving, nurturing, compassionate partner — someone who can help you navigate the rough seas.

Addendum: After writing this, I am struck again by the importance of opening my vulnerable self to a woman who truly knows how to nurture. Perhaps everyone carries that capacity in some dormant form, but some possess it with a rare, almost sacred fluency. It becomes part of my own complex calculus of love — alongside integrity, mutual understanding, and the quiet, essential art of tending to another's trembling heart.

A HARROWING MONTH

"The major difference between a thing that might go wrong and a thing that cannot possibly go wrong is that when a thing that cannot possibly go wrong goes wrong, it usually turns out to be impossible to get at or repair it." — Douglas Adams.

It began as a routine dermatological exam — the kind I've always taken seriously, with no denial mechanism to speak of. Early detection has been my religion. I had no idea that this ordinary appointment would detonate the most harrowing month I've had in years.

For several years, I'd asked my dermatologist about four small bumps on my left shoulder and arm. Each time, she dismissed them as nothing. This time, I asked her to remove one "just to check." She reluctantly agreed. Then, as she continued the exam, she paused at my right groin.

"What's this?" she asked.

"Probably a little jock itch," I said casually.

"Afraid not," she replied. "That's no jock itch."

Something in her tone — the certainty, the lack of hesitation — made my stomach drop.

"Then what do you think it is?"

Without missing a beat, she said, "It looks like Mycosis Fungoides."

A wave of nausea washed over me. I sat down, dizzy. "Come on," I said, "that's a rare, fatal condition."

"It's not that rare," she said, "and in this early patch stage, it won't kill you. It can be controlled for many years."

Her confidence felt like a blow. She ordered a biopsy and left the room. Her physician assistant returned to take samples from both the groin and the shoulder. That was the last time I saw her that day.

For her, it was just another case. For me, it was a nightmare.

I walked out of the office in a daze, hearing only that they would call in a week to ten days. Ten days of purgatory.

I first learned about Mycosis Fungoides in 1962, during a pathology lecture by Dr. Archides Rivlin. Back then, it was considered invariably fatal. I can still see the page in my lecture notes. The notes are gone, but the memory remains — and so does the internet. For the next week, I immersed myself in everything I could find. The more I read, the more terrified I became.

I kept replaying her tone, her certainty. Where was her sensitivity? Did she think she was talking to a colleague on rounds about a patient in the next room? If I had been the dermatologist, I would have said, "Let's biopsy it — it could be several things." Instead, she went straight to the rarest, most ominous diagnosis, delivered with the bedside manner of a chainsaw.

The groin biopsy came back "consistent with Mycosis Fungoides." The shoulder bump came back "possibly MF." My anxiety skyrocketed. She then casually mentioned that the shoulder lesion might be a "follicular form of MF," something I had never heard of. She removed the remaining bumps and told me she had trained with the world expert in Pittsburgh — as if that were supposed to reassure me.

Then she went on vacation for several weeks.

I was left alone with my fear.

I sent the pathology reports to Dr. Daniel Rivlin, the son of the very professor who taught me about MF fifty years ago. He told me the diagnosis was "complicated and sketchy," that many conditions mimic MF, and that he only leaned toward MF because my dermatologist had written "rule out MF" on the requisition. He ordered gene-rearrangement studies — the gold standard — but they would take three weeks.

Waiting was torture.

I used the steroid cream she prescribed, but covered it with antifungal ointment because steroids can worsen fungal infections. A retired dermatologist examined me and reassured me it was unlikely to be MF. I clung to that.

Then came the surreal moment in the movie theater. I was watching *Not Fade Away* when James Gandolfini's character announced at the dinner table, "The doctor told me I have cancer — they call it Mycosis Fungoides." I stared at my friends in disbelief. I had never heard MF mentioned in a film. The timing felt like a cosmic prank.

The remaining shoulder biopsies came back negative. The lymph node under my arm — present for seven years — had not grown. These were good signs. But the gene-rearrangement results were still pending.

Finally, after more than three weeks, the call came. The office hesitated to give me the results because the doctor hadn't signed off. I insisted. They read them: polyclonal, not monoclonal. Not MF.

Relief flooded me. I called my daughter and close friends. We all exhaled.

When my dermatologist returned, I went to get hard copies of the report. She hadn't seen them yet. When she did, she invited me in, reassured me I was "out of the woods," and estimated an 80 percent chance the rash would never return. Then she hugged me and apologized.

I accepted the apology, though part of me wondered whether I should. Was it sincere? Or was it a perfunctory gesture to cover her tracks? I wasn't sure.

What I do know is this: when you've been hit on the head repeatedly with a hammer, it feels indescribably good when it stops.

I also learned — again — how often medical "authorities" speak with conviction while standing on clay feet. The deterioration of bedside manners, the erosion of empathy, and the triumph of ego over humanity — it's disheartening. Medicine has become a culture where convenience and speed often trump care and precision.

Will I stay with her? I tend to forgive, to give people room to grow. But I'm not sure this is a growth issue. It may be a character issue — and character rarely changes.

Addendum: Forgiving this kind of medical misstep is difficult because it strikes at the heart of trust. As a physician, I know the importance of precision, humility, and care. A hug and an apology were steps in the right direction, but the wound was still raw. In the end, it was time to move on — to find a dermatologist with more empathy, more calibration, and less cavalier certainty.

SATISFACTION

"Satisfaction lies in the effort, not in the attainment; full effort is a full victory."
— Mahatma Gandhi.

For the past six months, I've had little desire to write. Chronic, unrelenting pain has a way of shutting down the creative impulse. My neurologist tells me I'm not yet a candidate for lumbar spinal surgery. I've seriously considered it, but he insists I be patient — that time will resolve what feels, at the moment, unresolvable.

Pain is one problem. The other is meaning.

Retirement without golf has left me startled by how dependent I've become on this maddening, beautiful, physical, mental game to structure my days, socialize my time, and give me a clear, open-ended goal. Golf was my compass. Without it, I've been drifting.

Today, for the first time in months, I practiced my short game — chipping, pitching, putting, sand shots. No full swings. And to my surprise, I felt happy. Revitalized. The small satisfactions — correcting a bad shot, feeling the club connect cleanly, watching a ball roll true — stirred something in me. It was enough to make me want to write again.

I remember a colleague, thirty years my senior, telling me early in my career that a life without goals has no meaning. At the time, I understood him intellectually, but emotionally, it didn't land. As my mother used to say, "You can't put an old head on a young person." Now that I'm the age he was then, the truth of his words has finally clicked. Without goals, there is no satisfaction, no fulfillment, no purpose.

Perhaps the lesson is this: the incremental pleasures of golf — the small improvements, the patient corrections — can be applied to my sciatic pain. Adjust the stretching. Modify the exercises. Vary the activities. Persevere. The process is not so different from improving a golf game: slow, frustrating, humbling, but ultimately rewarding.

Maybe this is one of the inevitable aspects of being human — learning to adapt to the body's breakdowns, to accept the limitations that come with age, and to find new ways to pursue pleasure when the old ways falter. I think of a dear friend who became a quadriplegic after a diving accident. Years later, he showed me — with enormous pride — how he could make himself a burger, use a computer, and drive his customized van. Each accomplishment was a victory. Each small success carried meaning.

I need to shift my thinking in that direction. To reframe this period not as a loss, but as a goal-oriented challenge. To move away from sadness and dissatisfaction and toward adaptation.

Golf may become part of my past, just as tennis, running, and skiing have. If so, I'll need to find something else — hiking, biking, swimming, or some pastime I haven't yet discovered — that keeps me engaged in a game worth playing.

Time will tell. If the pain worsens, interferes with sleep, and drags me back into that helpless state of agony, I'll let the surgeon do his work. But if, as my neurologist believes, a tincture of time and a reservoir of patience bring me back into the game, that will be deeply satisfying.

Addendum: This brief essay speaks about the difficulty of living with chronic pain and the challenge of finding satisfaction in the midst of it. Pain narrows the world. But with patience — and more patience — small efforts can accumulate into meaningful change. I'm choosing to trust my wise neurologist's perspective, and to trust myself enough to keep making the effort, one small victory at a time.

REGAINED SIMPLICITY

"Our life is frittered away by detail… Simplify, simplify." — Henry David Thoreau.

Life accumulates complexity the way a shoreline gathers debris — slowly, relentlessly, and often without our noticing. College, graduate school, medical training, decades of patient care. Marriage, children, the intricate choreography of family life. The ravages of aging, financial setbacks, and the deaths of loved ones. Layer upon layer of responsibility, expectation, and emotional weight. At some point, we look up and wonder: What actually matters? What remains when the scaffolding of obligation falls away?

My mother — wise, stubborn, and recently gone — used to say that the secret was to make life as simple as possible. A deceptively difficult task when you're striving, proving, and achieving. We spend so much of our lives trying to demonstrate something to others, or to ourselves, as if the universe is keeping score. And then, after the goals are reached, after the trophies are on the shelf, after the applause fades — what then?

I find myself questioning how much of life is truly chosen. How much is simply the result of being in a particular psychological state at a particular moment, our moods and biochemistry shifting beneath us like weather fronts. We imagine ourselves as rational agents making deliberate choices, but more often we are carried by currents we barely understand. The right place, the right time, the right internal climate — and suddenly a decision is made.

Now, for the first time in decades, I have arrived at a place of complete autonomy. No obligations other than those I choose to create. I could pick up my conga drums and reclaim the skills I spent years cultivating. I could practice Argentine Tango, though dancing alone quickly loses its charm. I could bike, swim, or push myself into better shape, but I already worked out this morning and feel no urge to burn more calories. I could pay bills, but nothing is overdue. I could call an old friend, but I'm not in the mood for conversation. I could watch a movie, read a book, study a language — but none of it calls me.

What I want, right now, is simply to write. Seeing where the writing takes me. To understand how I've arrived at this strange, unburdened state — a simplicity so unfamiliar it feels like an altered state of consciousness. For most of my life, there was always a task, a goal, a responsibility pulling me forward. Now there is nothing except golf — the one endless pursuit that still structures the vast open space I've stumbled into.

My daughter is doing well. My mother is gone. My friends are living their own lives. There is no significant woman to share my days with. Life has become straightforward, almost startlingly so — unless I begin to question it. The moment I think I should be somewhere else, doing something else, the simplicity evaporates, and conflict rushes in.

This state of mind reminds me of early childhood — preschool days when the world was unstructured, when time stretched out like an open field, when doing nothing felt natural. There is something Zen-like about it: a meditative stillness, a peaceful emptiness. I know it won't last. Life has a way of reasserting its complexity. But for now, I intend to savor it. Simplicity is a gift — fleeting, fragile, and worth celebrating while it's here.

Addendum: A complicated life can become addictive. The stress, the striving, the constant motion — they create a familiar rhythm, even a sense of identity. Letting go of that rhythm can feel frightening, as if idleness were a moral failing. Those internalized parental voices still whisper: *Don't be lazy. Don't be unproductive.* But once you taste the calmness of simplicity — the therapeutic quiet, the absence of pressure — it becomes clear that stepping into neutral now and then is not a failure. It is a form of wisdom.

A BREAK INTO THE VOID

"A thousand thoughts are lying within a man that he does not know till he takes up a pen to write." — William Makepeace Thackeray.

I sit here with nothing to write. No inspiration, no spark, no inner monologue pushing its way toward the page. The familiar stream of thoughts that usually ushers in an essay has gone silent. I don't know whether this is writer's block or simply the natural ebb in the rhythm of writing — the tide pulling back before it returns. Maybe if I keep typing, something will surface. Or maybe I'll sit here long enough to grow irritated, hit delete, and call it a day. For now, I'm just waiting — waiting for something evocative to stir.

I've just returned from a long, satisfying round of golf. Florida's summer heat can be punishing, but the camaraderie, the movement, the small triumphs and failures of the game gave me my social fix. Lunch with friends, a quick check of email, some newly downloaded music — and then the impulse to sit down and see if anything creative might emerge.

I have time. A great deal of it. Retirement offers an enormous sense of freedom — the ability to do whatever I want, whenever I want, with no schedule and no obligations. And yet, even after years of retirement, there are moments when I wonder how to structure my days in a way that feels meaningful. So, I sit here, trying to process what's going on in my head.

What makes me want to do this? Do others feel the same pull — the urge to stand at the edge of the void and try to coax something meaningful out of it? Fixing, reading, watching — none of it feels as challenging or as significant as writing. Writing is the act of making something out of nothing.

But perhaps the wiser move is to stop trying to fill the void and simply inhabit it. To sit with the experience of nothingness. To savor the rare flavor of an empty mind — a mind not busy interpreting, analyzing, or constructing meaning. Maybe floating in the void is the purest form of relaxation, peace, and harmony.

After a lifetime of using my mind to figure things out — or to create the illusion that I have — I'm beginning to see how much of that effort is a defense against helplessness. The helplessness of not knowing. The helplessness of being human. If we didn't assume we were supposed to understand everything, the anxiety of not understanding would evaporate.

Learning to live comfortably without comprehension is no small task for a psychiatrist. Our training elevates thought to a near-sacred status. When confronted with difficulty, our minds go into overdrive, generating interpretations to make sense of nonsense. It's a professional reflex — and a personal one.

Then we retire. The patients disappear. The mysteries of the human condition no longer arrive in fifty-minute increments. The mind, however, doesn't retire. It keeps sorting, analyzing, interpreting — and when there are no patients left, it turns inward. It applies its lifelong habits to family, friends, and, most effectively, oneself. Writing becomes the new consulting room. The page becomes the patient. And the process continues — using what I've learned rather than losing it.

Addendum: When I began this essay, I felt empty — a welcome, serendipitous breather from decades of cerebral overactivity. But familiarity is a powerful force. Before long, I found myself doing what I've always done: giving meaning to the day, shaping the void into something coherent, returning to the comfort zone of reflection. Whether it means much in the grand scheme of things is debatable. But it is, undeniably, what I do — and perhaps who I am.

RAGING OVER BAD LUCK

"The closest to being in control we will ever be is in that moment that we realize we're not." — Brian Kessler.

It seems absurd to become aggravated over something as trivial as a bad bounce in golf or an unlucky roll of the dice. Rationally, we know these moments are meaningless — random flickers of chance that any well-balanced person should be able to shrug off. And sometimes we do. Sometimes we even laugh at the fickle finger of fate pointing elsewhere.

But other times, we want to scream. Walk off the course. Throw the dice across the room. The rage feels disproportionate, childish, even embarrassing — yet unmistakably real.

Where does that reactivity come from? How do we go from being someone who can roll with life's punches to an irritable child on the verge of a tantrum because a ball took a bad hop?

It's the presupposition — often unconscious — that life should go the way we want it to go. Smooth fairways. Clear skies. Perfect shots. Dice that cooperate. No losses, only wins. A fantasy of control that belongs more to infancy than adulthood.

We know it's ridiculous. We know it's unrealistic. And yet, under certain conditions, we regress. Our emotions fly in the face of common sense.

I've come to believe that these outbursts rarely arise in isolation. They're the culmination of a slow buildup — health concerns, financial hits, relationship losses, the erosion of professional identity. When the essential pillars of life wobble, the psyche becomes sensitized. A trivial misfortune becomes the symbolic stand-in for everything else we can't control.

Imagine life is going well — work, love, play all in harmony — and then the stock market crashes, wiping out years of careful gains. A long-term relationship dissolves. The professional identity that once anchored you evaporates in retirement. Suddenly, that bad bounce on the 7th hole feels like a personal affront. The dice roll the wrong way, and it feels as if the universe is conspiring against you.

It's displacement — the helplessness we don't want to feel redirected toward something safe enough to rage at. It becomes a kind of magical thinking: *Lady Luck is out to get me.* A quasi-paranoid whisper: *What's coming next?*

Instead of grieving the real losses, we rage at the symbolic ones. We pound our chest like a gorilla trying to reclaim authority — authority we never truly had. But maybe the raging, like crying, is part of the grieving process. Maybe it's the psyche's way of metabolizing helplessness until the trivial misfortunes lose their power.

Eventually, if we're lucky, we come to terms with how little control we have over life. We adapt. We recalibrate. We learn to be content with the basics — the ability to walk, breathe, laugh, and still show up for the game.

But most of us only reach that level of wisdom when time is running down or running out.

Addendum: Someone once said that the irony of life is that by the time we're old enough to know our way around, we're not going anywhere. Maybe now that I've written this, the next time luck turns against me, I'll pause, breathe, and let the moment pass without theatrics. Perhaps I'll even chuckle. Writing it down has a way of accelerating the evolution — a small victory over the illusion of control.

THE MEANING OF WINNING AND LOSING

"The fear of losing is the flip side of the need to win… evolution doesn't favor losers." — Gene Bedell.

I've become an avid Miami Heat fan, swept up in the exhilaration of winning and the devastation of losing. These tight, breathless, down-to-the-wire games generate adrenaline surges that feel almost hazardous to my cardiac rhythm. It's astonishing how deeply a contest played by strangers can penetrate the psyche.

This isn't new. As a boy, I was a loyal Brooklyn Dodgers fan. I can still see myself at twelve, sitting in front of my small Philco black-and-white TV as Russ Hodges screamed, "THE GIANTS WIN THE PENNANT!" Bobby Thomson's home run — the shot heard 'round the world — shattered me. I spilled my Coke, cursed, and ran out of the house while my mother yelled, "What's the matter with you?" I wandered the neighborhood for hours, devastated.

Over the years, I've watched fans lose their minds — English soccer riots, American fans overturning cars, setting fires, brawling in the streets. What is that all about? What psychological machinery gets activated when our team loses?

In sports, politics, and life, the emotional stakes of winning and losing can be enormous. Golf, for example, is a master class in emotional volatility. Perfectionists suffer the most — believing, irrationally, that they should be better than they are. A bad shot feels like a personal insult. Tempers flare. It's road rage with a 7-iron.

Underlying it all is the fantasy that life should unfold smoothly — no bumps, no storms, no bad bounces. When that illusion collapses, we rage, despair, pound our chests, and shout at the gods. But the truth is painful: life unfolds as it wishes, not as we wish. Our rooting has no impact on the outcome. When our illusions of control disintegrate, it feels like a small psychic death — an unconscious metaphorical castration.

We cannot control our destiny, our loved ones, or our team's fate. The belief that we can is a grandiose, residual infantile fantasy — the omnipotence we once felt as infants screaming for the breast, believing our cries commanded the universe. That early helplessness, that vulnerable separateness, is so intolerable that we spend much of adulthood trying to ward it off.

We do it through games, gambling, sports, relationships, health obsessions — anything that gives us a fleeting sense of mastery. Winning becomes a symbolic triumph over helplessness. Losing becomes humiliation, fragility, exposure. To identify with a winning team is to feel large, proud, and powerful. To identify with a losing team is to feel small, ashamed, and out of control.

The belief seems to be that if we win often enough — in sports, in life, in love — we can magically protect ourselves from the uncontrollable. Illness, death, catastrophe — we try to outrun them through mastery. Beat the odds at craps, roulette, or the slot machines, and maybe we'll beat the Grim Reaper too. Narcotize ourselves with alcohol or drugs, and we inflate the illusion of power even further.

But ultimately, it all comes down to letting go of the fear of dying, relinquishing the need to control outcomes, and learning to flow with life rather than fight it. The Buddhists have it right: let things be as they are. If we can cultivate that stance — regardless of genetic predisposition — we can soften the adrenaline spikes that harm us.

Most of us want to mellow out eventually, even if it means sacrificing some of the exhilaration. Age helps. Loss helps. Life knocks us around enough that we begin to adopt our elders' philosophy: This too shall pass. So, what else is new?

But here's the paradox: we cannot simply choose to let go. Positive affirmations, cognitive reframing, mindfulness — they help, but they don't transform. True acceptance comes only through experience — through the repeated, painful lessons that life is what it is, regardless of our preferences. Yielding happens to us, not because of us. Resilience grows in the cracks.

The Miami Heat, after a three-year streak of near invincibility, has now stumbled. Losses pile up. Fans are forced to confront the illusion that the team — like all of us — is mortal. And yet, paradoxically, letting go sometimes opens the door to restoration. A team can rally just when it appears to be dying. So can we.

As the Buddhists say, "We'll see." Time tells the truth. If we live long enough, we may realize that our separateness — our tribal rooting for and against — is a kind of mental aberration that obstructs peace of mind and love. A world without preferences is a beautiful idea, but unlikely in a society built on competition.

Addendum: We live in a divide-and-conquer world, driven by consumerism and fragile egos desperate for armor. Our culture rewards aggression, narcissism, and tribalism far more than love, peace, or unity. Reversing that trend is ideal — but improbable. Perhaps it remains the domain of spiritual teachers, Eastern philosophers, and the idealistic flower children who once believed we could build a gentler world.

ABORTED VACATION

"Man plans, God laughs." — Yiddish Saying

I had been looking forward to this trip in a way I hadn't anticipated. Hiking in Switzerland — something I once loved and hadn't done in years — felt like a symbolic return to vitality, to movement, to the younger man who could climb mountains without thinking twice. I had booked the Engadin Valley, St. Moritz, Pontresina, and a final cultural immersion in Zurich. It felt like reclaiming a part of myself that had gone dormant.

I arrived at Miami International Airport two hours early, wanting to give my luggage every chance of making it to Zurich. I boarded the 5 PM flight to JFK with that quiet, anticipatory excitement that comes before a long-awaited adventure.

Then came the announcement: severe storms in New York. We would remain on the ground.

And remain we did — long enough for anxiety to begin its slow creep. I asked the crew to notify the Zurich connection to wait for us. They reassured me with that bland airline confidence: "If the weather is bad, they'll be delayed too." I didn't believe it. I was right. We reached the gate at 10:20 PM. The Zurich flight was gone.

Just like that, the trip began to unravel.

This was the last flight to Europe out of JFK. I scrambled to rebook, only to be told — in that maddening bureaucratic loop — that because this was a SkyMiles award, only SkyMiles could help. SkyMiles told me only JFK could help. JFK told me there were no seats to Zurich for two days. The best they could offer was Stuttgart, via Atlanta, arriving the next day. From there, I would be on my own to find my way to Zurich. And even then, who knew whether my luggage would follow.

By the time I imagined arriving in Zurich late Sunday afternoon, then taking a four-hour train to St. Moritz, exhausted and gearless, the trip had already died in my mind.

I asked them to put me on another airline. They refused. Weather delays meant they were only obligated to use Delta flights, all of which were sold out in peak summer.

So, I said, "Get me a hotel at JFK, re-route my luggage back to Miami, and I'm canceling this vacation."

It was 2:30 AM by the time I reached the Ramada after a train and shuttle ride. They had no rooms. My heart was skipping beats; the stress felt dangerous. The manager eventually found a miserable room with bed bugs. Sleep was impossible.

I returned to the airport, tried standby for the 8 AM flight — no luck. Waited for the 1 PM flight — got on — only to sit on the runway for three more hours because the cabin door wouldn't close.

When I finally arrived in Miami, my luggage was nowhere to be found. I filed a report. Five days passed. No luggage. No answers. No one at MIA or JFK seemed reachable.

And here's the part that surprised me: I unraveled.

Not dramatically. Not publicly. But internally, the way a man unravels when the illusion of control is stripped away. It wasn't just about the trip. It was about everything the trip represented: freedom, vitality, movement, the ability to plan and execute, the belief that life will cooperate if you do your part.

This fiasco exposed the fragility beneath that illusion.

Yes, it could always be worse — the plane could have crashed, a terrorist could have boarded, or I could have had a cardiac episode — but this was, without exaggeration, the worst travel experience of my life. And it hit me harder than it should have because it touched something deeper: the fear that life is becoming less predictable, less manageable, less within my grasp.

Then, finally, my luck turned. My luggage arrived from Zurich. The relief was instantaneous—Valium-like. A wave of calm washed over me. Amazing how deeply I let it get under my skin.

I wish I had a strategy to inoculate myself against this kind of stress. I know all the intellectual advice — I've given it to patients for decades: roll with the punches, accept what is, relinquish control, don't let "stuff" erode your peace of mind. Easier said than done.

I will not accept abuse from anyone — especially not a giant corporation. My next battle was getting my SkyMiles back. Delta insisted I was only entitled to the unused portion of the Europe ticket and that I must pay for the Miami–JFK turnaround. I refused. I contacted the Department of Transportation, Action Line, and anyone else who might help.

And wouldn't you know — once Action Line intervened, Delta suddenly found its heart. A full apology. Full reimbursement. All miles restored. Amazing what a metaphorical two-by-four of public pressure can accomplish.

I think I'll write myself a prescription for a travel break to recover from this absurd saga.

Addendum: Life ambushes us with its uncontrollable features, often when we least expect it. We are never fully prepared. I wish I were. Perhaps the only real antidote is to become more philosophical, less reactive, and not take it all so personally. Acceptance seems to win over resistance — eventually — as life drags us through its stress-induced strengthening process.

REFLECTIVE TRANSITIONS ON COMING HOME

"Home is a place you grow up wanting to leave and grow old wanting to get back to." — John Ed Pearce.

For a long time, I thought I would never return. Life can cast us so far adrift that finding our way back — to the place where the heart feels most at ease — becomes an arduous, complicated journey. Thomas Wolfe famously wrote that you can't go home again. Perhaps he meant it metaphorically: you can never return to the internal or external world you once inhabited. But if you can reconcile the tension between what was and what is, coming home can be an extraordinary experience.

I spent the first fourteen years of my life in Manhattan — the great Big Apple, with its cultural electricity, intellectual hum, and the simple pleasures of street-side hot dogs and potato knishes. My world was stickball, punchball, stoopball, and the endless playgrounds of Central and Riverside Parks. We fed pigeons, chased squirrels, and jumped on the subway to Ebbets Field or the Polo Grounds to watch the Dodgers and Giants battle it out. It was the only world I knew, and it fit me like a second skin.

Then, in the fall of 1953, my mother decided — unilaterally — that we would move to Miami Beach. I felt uprooted, disoriented, and convinced my life would never be the same. And it wasn't. It was better.

Miami Beach, in its heyday, was a revelation. Palm trees, beaches, resorts, and weather that felt like a perpetual summer vacation. Being licensed to drive at fourteen was a teenage dream. Museums and cultural institutions were easy sacrifices for a boy intoxicated by sun, sand, and freedom.

The real challenge was making new friends. Miami Beach High was a small, eclectic mix of kids — children of hotel owners, mobsters, lawyers, doctors, and struggling single mothers. But they all shared one thing: they knew how to have fun. We water-skied, deep-sea fished, skin-dived, and spearfished. We held nighttime beach parties behind the old Firestone Estate, where the Fontainebleau now stands. We swam and high-dived at the grand old hotels — the McFadden Deauville, the Roney Plaza, the Robert Richter — all gone now, replaced by soulless modern structures.

At night, we cruised Collins Avenue in convertibles, picking up young tourists and hosting cabana parties. We attended the openings of the Fontainebleau and the Eden Roc, and, through well-connected friends, we watched Frank, Sammy, Dean, and Elvis. Life was one long, intoxicating party.

We rubbed elbows with gangsters, gamblers, bookies, pimps, and their call girls. Through my friendship with Michael Dundee, I met boxing legends — Cassius Clay, Willie Pep, Jake LaMotta, Willie Pastrano. One unforgettable Friday night at the Miami Beach Auditorium, I shook hands with Rocky Marciano, Joe Louis, and Jack Dempsey — whose hand felt like a catcher's mitt carved from granite.

We slipped into clubs with altered IDs, listened to George Shearing with Herbie Mann and Candido, wandered into the Night Owl with its Sinatra-only jukebox and haze of marijuana, and danced to Pupi Campo, Tito Puente, and Luis Verona. My love for Latin rhythms deepened during a summer in Cuba in 1956.

We ate at Piccolo's, Wolfe's, Juniors, and Pumpernick's. We worked as beach and cabana boys, parked cars at Ciro's, the Latin Quarter, Copa City, and the Beachcomber. We met Milton Berle, Jimmy Durante, Sophie Tucker, Tony Bennett, Duke Ellington, Ella Fitzgerald, and Count Basie. We drove to Overtown to hear Miles Davis and Ramsey Lewis at the Sir John Hotel. It was a Hollywood movie come to life.

High school friends became fraternity brothers at the University of Florida, then classmates at the University of Miami School of

Medicine. Twelve years of continuity created bonds that felt like family.

In 1966, after my internship at Jackson Memorial, it was time to move again — this time for specialty training. I had no idea I would be gone for thirty-four years.

Residency at Columbia Presbyterian reawakened my intellectual and cultural life. My stint with the U.S. Public Health Service led to research at the National Institute of Mental Health. I eventually settled into a long career practicing and teaching psychiatry at Georgetown in Washington, D.C. — a city of politics, power, and diplomacy. Psychoanalysis deepened my understanding of myself and others. It was enriching but demanding.

By the time I approached sixty, I had watched too many friends and patients die too young, burdened by regrets. No one ever said, "I wish I had spent more time at the office." They all said the same thing: "I didn't spend enough time seeing the world or being with the people I love."

I was still healthy enough to choose differently.

I tried to recreate the carefree joy of my Miami years — marathons, ski trips, tennis, conga drumming, Mambo, Argentine Tango — but it never fully offset the pressure of a busy psychiatric practice. Collecting African antiquities brought solace. Writing a screenplay brought laughter back into my life. But I needed more. I needed lightness. I needed home.

I considered Marin County, Santa Fe, Aspen, and Crested Butte — but my heart wasn't going west. My daughter was in Manhattan. My ninety-year-old mother was in Bethesda. My closest friends were scattered along the East Coast. The die was cast.

And so, I returned.

Now, back in Miami, I find myself reconnecting with the place that shaped me. Some say you must remember the past to build a future. Perhaps that's true. At sixty-five, I'm enjoying the freedom of not knowing what I'll do from moment to moment. No schedule. Minimal responsibility. The luxury of choosing — or not choosing.

Am I bored? Only when I resist where I am. Boredom is the conflict between the present and the imagined elsewhere. When I accept the moment, boredom dissolves.

Our priorities shift with age. Youth value fun. Adulthood values accomplishment, responsibility, and productivity. Now, in this later chapter, I find myself returning to the youthful priority of joy — not irresponsibility, but freedom.

Ashley Montague wrote that playfulness, creativity, and exploration are the keys to "dying young as late in life as possible." So, I wake up, have a leisurely breakfast, read the paper, check email for jokes and news, go to the gym, schmooze with friends, and then decide what I feel like doing. Golf. A boat ride. A nap. A book. Volunteering. Maybe even working again — not out of obligation, but desire.

It's not easy to clear the mental clutter and sit in the void. But if we can do it — even briefly — it taps the creative unconscious and guides us toward what soothes the soul. Whatever choice emerges is made freely, without conflict. It feels, in its own way, like coming home.

Addendum: In writing this, I noticed how I de-emphasized the disappointments and losses that shape our humanity. I've had my share of painful, terrifying experiences. Much of what drives our mood and behavior operates unconsciously, through habitual sorting principles. To keep my spirits high — and my golf score low — I'm learning to shift my focus toward the good shots, making them more important than the bad ones. The same applies to life. The pleasant memories I've revisited here give me hope — for the future, for joy, and for whatever time remains.

GOLF AS A METAPHOR OF CHARACTER

"If you wish to hide your character, do not play golf." — Percy Boomer.

Character is the aggregate of traits that form a person's nature — the patterns of behavior, the quirks, the integrity, the blind spots, the oddities. And golf, that maddening game of jubilation and despair, is one of the most reliable psychological X-rays ever invented. It reveals who we are with the precision of a Rorschach test and the candor of a Sodium Amytal interview.

If a father wants to know who his future son-in-law really is, he should take him out for a round of golf — preferably on a course with plenty of water and bunkers. If an employer wants to understand a potential hire, forget the résumé; take him to the links. Within a few holes, the truth emerges.

Golf, like life, has rules. How we follow them — or don't — tells a story. There are no shortcuts to mastery. It requires patience, discipline, humility, and the willingness to learn from those who know more. Yet golfers often justify bending the rules: "I'm only a beginner," "I need the practice," "What's the big deal if I take a few Mulligans?" It's fine — as long as we don't delude ourselves into believing we earned our score honestly.

Below are some universal character types that show up on the golf course. Few people fit neatly into one category; most of us are a blend. To have none of these traits is admirable but dull. To have many is interesting but disordered. Read with humor, not self-condemnation — this is meant to amuse, not diagnose.

The Dependent Golfer

Terrified of being alone, they cling to you like a barnacle. Once, an elderly man asked to join me. After one hole, he lost sight of his ball and snapped, "Can't you see I'm legally blind?" He demanded I stand beside him at all times. If I drifted even a few feet, he erupted:

"Where the hell were you?" For a man claiming to be blind, he hit fairways with suspicious accuracy. Go figure.

The Depressive Golfer

One bad shot and they spiral into despair. "I give up. I'll never play this rotten game again." They speak in absolutes: "I always slice," "I'm worthless." After everyone reassures them, I sometimes agree: "You're right — you're the worst golfer I've ever played with." They instantly protest: "What are you talking about? I'm not!" Their gloom is contagious.

The Paranoid Golfer

Everything is someone else's fault. "That groundskeeper distracted me." "I've been robbed!" "Someone's messing with my game." They glare suspiciously, brood, and sometimes stare at you until your swing collapses — which, to their satisfaction, confirms their worldview.

The Obsessive-Compulsive Golfer

Golf attracts them like moths to flame, doctors, lawyers, executives — perfectionists who cannot tolerate failure. Golf humbles them mercilessly. Four pars and a birdie mean nothing if the next hole is a bogey. They rage, toss clubs, and condemn themselves. They follow rules with religious fervor and expect you to do the same. They can be rigid, intolerant, and exhausting — unless they learn to lighten up.

The Passive-Aggressive Golfer

They show up late, forget to show up at all, or arrive with excuses: "Traffic was terrible," "My alarm didn't go off." They sulk between holes, pout like children, and sometimes refuse to finish the round.

The Narcissistic Golfer

Grandiose, entitled, and allergic to criticism. They want special treatment — three-foot gimmies, exemptions from rules, applause for mediocrity. They can be charming, but their self-preoccupation is relentless. They will sabotage your game if it feeds their ego.

The Histrionic Golfer

Flamboyant, dramatic, seductive. They crave admiration: "You're so strong," "You hit it so far." They flirt, exaggerate, and seek reassurance. Precision and discipline are not their strengths.

The Schizoid or Schizotypal Golfer

Rare on the course — golf is too social. If you do encounter one, expect silence, eccentricity, and minimal reciprocity. Compliments fall into a void. You may feel the "willies," that eerie sense of wanting to jump out of your skin.

The Avoidant Golfer

They desperately want a connection but fear criticism. They need constant reassurance and unconditional acceptance. They usually play only with family or a trusted friend.

The Borderline Golfer

Argumentative one moment, depressed the next, then empty. They drain you emotionally. Fortunately, golf requires more ego strength than they typically possess, so they are rare on the course.

The Sociopathic Golfer

They lie, cheat, manipulate, and boast about fraudulent scores. They hustle you into bets and may threaten you if you confront them. Think of Tony Soprano with a 9-iron. They usually play among themselves.

The Masochist and the Sadist

The masochist seeks humiliation — golf provides plenty. The sadist enjoys inflicting pain — only a true masochist chooses him as a partner.

The So-Called Normal Golfer

A rare species. Think Ernie Els, Freddie Couples, Retief Goosen — calm, gracious, unflappable. Were they lobotomized? Medicated? Or simply blessed with the perfect genetic constitution for golf? They are the saints of the sport — the ideal we strive for but rarely achieve.

The Larger Metaphor

Golf mirrors life. It confronts us with unfairness, bad bounces, unpredictable obstacles, and the brutal reality that we must play the ball as it lies. We compensate, adapt, focus on the present, learn from mistakes, and let go of disappointment.

What keeps us coming back is not masochism. It's the deep, hardwired desire to play honestly — to face ourselves without shortcuts. Every stroke, like every action in life, is unchangeable. Integrity matters.

It is painful to face our limitations. It is tempting to cut corners. But if we endure the discomfort, satisfaction emerges — not from perfection, but from effort. Golf teaches that accomplishment lies in the process, not the outcome. Dignity and credibility come from giving our best with integrity. Expect nothing. Hope freely. Take what you get. Play it as it lies. Life operates the same way.

Addendum: Whenever I write in this instructive tone, I realize how much I yearn to internalize what I'm teaching. My own characterological quirks interfere with both my life and my golf game. In medical school, we learned by "seeing one, doing one, teaching one." Writing is a form of teaching — and teaching is how we transform. Once we put our thoughts into dialogue, the odds of change increase. I hope the golf gods are listening.

INTEGRITY AT ITS BEST

"Always do right. This will gratify some people and astonish the rest." — Mark Twain.

For my sixty-fifth birthday, I wanted nothing extravagant — just a return to one of life's simple, perfect rituals: taking the Flying Cloud ferry from Hyannis to Nantucket, renting bikes, circling the island on a forty-mile ride, lunch at the Summer House in Sconset, a leisurely walk through town, and finally, a mixed-swirl frozen yogurt at Stars while sitting on the wharf overlooking the harbor. A day of uncomplicated pleasure.

The plan unfolded smoothly — until fate decided to add its own twists.

We boarded the 8 AM ferry, each with our Cingular-served Nokia phones clipped to our belts. When my significant other stepped off the boat, she unknowingly left her phone behind in the washroom. She didn't realize it until we'd completed the first leg of our ride to Madaket and back.

"Where did you last see it?" I asked. She looked stunned, perplexed. We retraced our steps mentally — the boat, the bike shop, and the drug store. No clarity. I called her number. No answer. I called Cingular to suspend her service.

We backtracked physically this time — drug store, bike shop, Steamship Authority's lost-and-found. Nothing. They told us to wait for the ferry's return. When the first crewmember stepped off, I asked if he'd found a phone. Without a word, he pointed to a small metal intercom box. Perched on top was the phone.

It felt surreal — a small miracle of honesty. We exhaled, relieved, and resumed our day.

We biked to Sconset, had a leisurely lunch at the Summer House, wandered through the village, then pushed hard along the Milestone path back toward town. At the rotary, a large red truck stopped to give us the right of way. I waved in appreciation, and we continued.

Moments later, I realized my own phone had fallen off my belt clip.

The odds of finding it felt microscopic. Still, we turned around and began retracing our route. Suddenly, my S.O.'s phone rang.

"Jack — someone is calling me from your phone."

We stopped, startled. "How could he know to call you?" I asked.

She relayed the story: "It's the guy in the red truck. He said he saw your phone fall when we crossed in front of him. He yelled, but we didn't hear. He picked it up and wants to meet us back at the rotary."

We rode back. A young African American man pulled up in the red truck, stepped out, and held my phone in the air. I reached for my wallet, offering a sizable reward. He looked genuinely surprised.

"No, no," he said. "It was a pleasure to help you." He refused the money.

I shook his hand firmly, looked him in the eye, and said, "I deeply appreciate what you did — the effort, the time, and most of all, the integrity you showed today."

He smiled warmly and drove off.

I stood there stunned. It felt like I had stepped into the Twilight Zone — a moment so pure, so unexpected, that it suspended the usual cynicism of daily life.

Who was this selfless young man? In New York, Washington, or Miami, I doubted the story would have unfolded this way. When I told our host's wife in Mashpee, she smiled knowingly.

"That's the difference that makes the difference up here," she said. "Integrity is more the norm than the exception."

It made me wonder why I wasn't spending more time in a place where such decency seemed to be woven into the cultural fabric.

Later, I realized how he'd known to call us — the last two numbers dialed on my phone were my S.O.'s and Cingular's. The Twilight Zone dissolved, but the awe remained.

I found myself hoping — perhaps naïvely — that our country's moral fiber might be moving in that direction. After 9/11, for a brief moment, it felt like it was. But the moment passed for most. Not for him.

Addendum: Writing this piece reminded me that this young man's action embodies the core of my ego ideal. Integrity is the highest-level criterion — the foundation of trust, love, and any long-lasting, healthy relationship. Without it, nothing holds. With it, everything becomes possible.

MY BEST FRIEND — WHAT DOES THAT MEAN?

C.S. Lewis once wrote that to the ancients, friendship was *"the happiest and most fully human of all loves; the crown of life and the school of virtue."* The older I get, the more I understand what he meant.

My *best friend* is tossed around casually, but when you stop and examine it, the meaning becomes far more complex. Is it reserved for one singular person? Or can it apply to several extraordinary individuals across a lifetime? I've used the term for more than one person, but today I'm thinking about the friend who occupies that role in my life right now — the one I speak to most often, laugh with most easily, cry with when needed, and get annoyed at without fear of retaliation or rejection. The one who shows up when the chips are down. That, to me, is my best friend.

But friendship evolves. Just as our criteria for choosing a mate shift over time, so do the qualities we seek in a friend. Childhood friendships are built on proximity and play. Adult friendships are built on shared values, emotional safety, and the ability to hold each other's truths without judgment. The friendships that endure — the ones that deepen over decades — become quasi-familial. They hold our history.

Mutual respect, reciprocity, and the willingness to share both joys and tragedies create a texture that only time can weave. And trust — the sacred trust of holding each other's private world in confidence — is the backbone. Betray that, and the friendship becomes something else entirely.

In an ideal world, one's mate would also be one's best friend. But life doesn't always cooperate. Many people — single, divorced, widowed — rely on friends or siblings to help them navigate the daily challenges and existential loneliness that inevitably arise. Anyone who claims life isn't difficult is living in an altered reality.

With that in mind, let me talk about my best friend, Bill.

We met in 1957 as college freshmen, became fraternity brothers, and after graduation in 1961, went our separate ways — medical school for me, dental school for him. In 1968, we found ourselves reunited at Columbia Presbyterian Medical Center, both in residency training. Since then, our lives have been intertwined — with and without our respective partners.

I also have another best friend, Freddie, who is more like a brother than a friend. We go back to kindergarten at PS 9 in Manhattan, 1944 or maybe even 1943. A lifetime of connection. But Fred lives in New York, and Bill lives in Miami, where I am now. Geography favors frequency, and frequency deepens bonds. Still, I visit Fred two or three times a year, and our kinship remains profound.

Bill and I are both retired now. He's remarried, with grandchildren. I remain divorced, with a daughter who has chosen a life without marriage or children. Yet Bill and I talk often, meet often, and share a rhythm that has been decades in the making.

In the old days, we took ski trips together. When Jeanie entered his life, the three of us skied as a team. A few years ago, they invited me to Alta, Utah, knowing my significant other doesn't ski and knowing my left leg had weakened after failed back and knee surgeries. They encouraged me anyway. I went. I skied. Not like the old days, but enough to feel alive. Their empathy, generosity, and calibration to my sadness made the trip meaningful.

Loyalty, dependability, affection, and availability have infused our friendship for years. We've shared crises, offered advice, or simply hung out without ceremony. We sailed Biscayne Bay for hours, letting the autopilot steer while we pondered life's imponderables one moment and laughed uncontrollably the next. We exchanged jokes on ski lifts, followed each other down mogul fields, and waited at the top of mountains like two overgrown kids, savoring the last run of the day.

When I lived in D.C., I often flew down for long weekends, always welcomed as a houseguest. Bill came up to D.C. only a few times — once to avoid being in town when his ex-wife got married, and another time with Jeanie and his sons for a family trip. Our children, when together, slipped easily into the comfort of shared history.

I remember one day on a sailboat — Bill, me, my daughter, and his two sons — when a 1957 doo-wop song blasted from the radio. Bill and I instantly sang along, channeling our teenage selves. The kids stared, stunned, then burst into laughter. It was a moment of pure generational continuity.

There is a rhythmic synchronicity that defines the best friendship. A shared wavelength. An ease. Some people never reach that level — they remain acquaintances, pleasant but slightly off-key. Others become lifelong companions.

Male friendship, however, carries its own complications. Unlike women, men often fear emotional intimacy with other men. The anxiety of appearing "too close" can inhibit vulnerability. Henning Bech, the Danish sociologist, wrote that the more a man tries to assure himself a friendship isn't homosexual, the more anxious he becomes — until the friendship becomes impossible.

Many men confine their conversations to sports, business, politics, and women — safe topics that avoid emotional exposure. But Bill and I can talk about anything. Depth doesn't threaten us. Vulnerability doesn't trigger fear.

I believe the men most afraid of closeness are those who have suppressed the desire for deep male friendship. When the urge to bond is proportional to the fear, intimacy becomes impossible.

I'm grateful that both Bill and Fred are secure enough in themselves to maintain deep, long-term friendships with me. As an only child, I've had to create my own surrogate siblings. Without them, the past becomes a private museum with no witnesses. With them, my life remains anchored in shared reality.

And then, unexpectedly, life surprised me with a new friend: Pete.

Rough around the edges, muscular even in his late sixties, intimidating at first glance — but beneath that exterior lies a gentle, loyal, deeply sensitive family man. After a successful Wall Street career, he now mentors friends and shares stories that are legendary in our circle. He would have been a formidable protector in my youth; now he is a source of laughter, perspective, and unexpected warmth.

Pete's friendship reminds me that the capacity for connection doesn't diminish with age — it evolves. He complements the long-standing bonds I've cherished for decades. He brings new energy, new stories, and new meanings. In many ways, he embodies the essence of a best friend: loyal, present, and unafraid of vulnerability.

Addendum: Deep friendships are among the most important aspects of life. They must be nourished, not taken for granted. Those with strong family ties have built-in anchors. Those of us without siblings rely on friends to keep us from dissolving into obscurity. They hold our memories, our stories, our truths. They keep us alive in ways that matter.

THE ORIGIN OF A HOBBY — TRUTH OR FICTION?

"The happiness of a man in this life does not consist in the absence but the mastery of his passions." — Alfred Lord Tennyson.

Hobbies — those curious clusters of activities we pursue for solace, stimulation, and pleasure — often appear to outsiders as random collections of interests. But their origins are rarely random. A local magazine once contacted me after hearing about my unusual trio of passions: collecting African antiquities, immersing myself in Afro-Cuban music, playing conga drums, and dancing to the rhythms of that culture. They wanted to know how such a constellation came to be.

The truth is, I'm not entirely sure myself.

My mother told me that as an infant, I was highly responsive to music in the crib. Perhaps we inherit certain "genetic magnets" — invisible pulls toward particular sounds, colors, textures, and forms. Growing up in Manhattan and later Miami — both hubs of Afro-Cuban music and dance — may have stirred something already latent in me.

In 1956, a high school classmate invited me to spend a few months in Cuba with his family. That trip changed everything. I was immersed in a culture where rhythm was not an accessory but a heartbeat. I bought a small set of bongos and taught myself to play, blissfully unaware of how much I didn't know. I danced and listened to the great Cuban bands — Benny Moré, Orquesta Aragón, Sonora Matancera with Celia Cruz, Conjunto Chappottín, El Chocolate, Cachao. Their music seeped into my bones.

Back in Miami, I graduated from high school and parlayed my newfound skills into a part-time job teaching dance at the newly opened Eden Roc Hotel. Summers in the Catskills exposed me to Machito and Tito Rodriguez. In Manhattan, I made pilgrimages to the Palladium — the Mecca of mambo mania — and danced at the Lido Beach clubs. I moved to the rhythms of La Playa Sextet, Tito Puente,

Johnny Pacheco, Larry Harlow, Charlie and Eddie Palmieri, Willie Colón, and Ray Barretto. The music was everywhere, and I couldn't get enough.

Then life shifted. I graduated from medical school, became a psychiatrist, and moved to Washington, D.C. Around 1970, I stumbled into the world of African sculpture. A few visits to the Museum of African Art, a friendship with a curator, and an introduction to Warren Robbins — the museum's founder — ignited a new passion. I devoured books, journals, and catalogs. I bid at auctions, visited dealers and collectors around the world, and slowly developed an eye for authenticity and quality. As a psychiatrist, I found the traditional art rich with cultural symbols and metaphorical narratives — visual attempts to impose order and meaning on a chaotic world.

Years later, my significant other surprised me with a two-hour conga lesson for my birthday. That gift reopened a door I didn't realize had been closed. I began flying from D.C. to New York once a month, venturing into Spanish Harlem for intensive lessons. I videotaped each session, studied the tapes obsessively, and returned for more. I listened to the great congueros — Chano Pozo, Tata Güines, Changuito, Patato Valdés — and marveled at the virtuosity of Giovanni Hidalgo, Richie Flores, and Daniel Ponce.

Then came the concert that tied everything together. The State Department brought Los Muñequitos de Matanzas — a legendary Afro-Cuban rumba group — to perform. I watched the rumberos clap out the guaguancó rhythm, take turns singing, dancing, and playing the quinto and tumba. Something in me recognized it instantly. It felt like coming home — familiar, comforting, inexplicably mine.

The common denominator of all these passions is their African root. Which raises the question: Why would a Caucasian, non-Latino male feel such a deep affinity for Africana?

I don't know. I can only speculate.

Psychiatrists speculate for a living — though I often wish for a blood test or X-ray to explain the mind's mysteries. Some, like Brian Weiss of *Many Lives, Many Masters*, might suggest that in a previous life I was African — perhaps even a shamanic healer, not so different from a psychiatrist. Maybe my genetic imperative has been whispering all along, drawing me toward African art, Afro-Cuban music, and dance because they feel like home.

How do I know that, Jack? I don't. But it makes as much sense as anything else I could invent.

Addendum: Do we ever truly know why we're drawn to the things we love? I certainly don't. We create stories, believe them, revise them, discard them, and create new ones. So, I'll keep the shamanic-healer theory — not because I'm convinced it's true, but because it feels right. And sometimes, that's enough.

ONCE UPON A MAMBO

"And those who were seen dancing were thought to be insane by those who could not hear the music." — Friedrich Nietzsche.

During the 1950s, New York and Miami were sanctuaries for the mambo lover — temples of rhythm where the clave ruled, and the body obeyed. I was a young, impressionable adolescent then, and I quickly discovered that being a decent dancer worked wonders with high-school girls. I wasn't quarterback material, but I had a natural feel for music, and learning to mambo became my ticket into a world that otherwise felt out of reach. Yet beyond its social utility, the music itself — that pulsing, hypnotic sound from Cuba — moved me in ways I didn't yet understand.

In 1953, shortly after we moved to Miami Beach, I took an after-school job cleaning cabanas at the elegant Sans Souci Hotel. Next door, at the Saxony, I would watch Pérez Prado and his band ignite the room with their Latin rhythms. I had no idea then that Prado was one of the architects of the mambo craze sweeping the United States. I only knew that something in the music was speaking to me.

During my first year of college, I dated a young dance teacher who taught me enough to land a summer and holiday job teaching dance. Throughout college and my early medical school years, I worked at the Fontainebleau, Eden Roc, and Deauville — glamorous resorts where the Basha brothers and other great dancers held court. From 1959 to 1961, the Bashas moved to the studio next to Harry's American Bar at the Eden Roc. Working alongside Albert Basha and Al Gray exposed me to a level of mastery I didn't yet appreciate. In 1962, I worked with Luigi Doranzo at the Deauville, not knowing that forty-three years later, our paths would cross again.

This story is about the characters who stayed true to the original Cuban form — dancers who resisted the dilution and commercialization of the mambo. At the center is Luigi, an Italian American bricklayer who, through sheer passion and grit, became one of the finest mambo dancers alive. A protégé of the legendary Al Gray, Luigi absorbed Gray's style until the two were nearly indistinguishable. Some might dispute my claim that Luigi is the best — taste is subjective — but in my eyes, his elegance, improvisational genius, and intuitive relationship with the clave placed him in a class of his own. He is the Frank Sinatra of dance — smooth, effortless, and blessed with those piercing blue eyes.

For decades, while practicing psychiatry in Washington, D.C., I had little opportunity to dance. The city was too conservative, too restrained. Latin dancing was out of vogue. My only chances came during trips to Manhattan — Club Corso, Club Broadway — or in Miami at Harry's American Bar, the Jockey Club, or the occasional dive in Little Havana where authentic Charanga and Conjunto bands played.

When I retired and returned to Miami, I called an old mambo-dancing anesthesiologist and asked where the scene was. He told me Luis Varona had died — a loss to the dance world — but urged me to go to the Goldcoast Ballroom in Coconut Creek, where every Sunday from 5 to 8 PM, the old masters and rising stars gathered. I went. And I rediscovered a part of myself I thought I had lost.

Among the dancers was Frances, a superb New York transplant who knew everything about the scene. She and the legendary Walter Darien reintroduced me to Luigi. He remembered me from the Deauville Hotel — remembered that I was starting medical school, remembered that I taught dance during summers and holidays. I was stunned. And grateful.

Needing to get back into shape, I drove from Key Biscayne to the Millennium Ballroom in Hallandale for hours of fine-tuning with Luigi. My goal was simple: keep his style alive within my own.

At the Goldcoast, the great dancer and attorney John Lucchese told me, "You're a natural. Don't try to clone Luigi." I thanked him, but I knew better. I would incorporate what I could — and if I was lucky,

I'd clone at least parts of Luigi. When you're in the hands of a true master, you trust him. He sees what you cannot see. He teaches what you didn't know you needed. He refuses mediocrity. And I love him for it.

Luigi is more than a dancer — he's a character. While describing his journey from bricklayer to dance icon, he'll tug at the collar of his crisp white shirt and say proudly, "Once it was blue, now it's white." After his wife died, he withdrew from the scene, but coaxing him back to the Goldcoast has been one of my small contributions to the dance world. Watching him reconnect with admirers — young and old — has been gratifying.

But admiration has its price. "Everyone wants a piece of me," he says. And he's right. Women swarm him, tugging at him for a dance, even when his knees ache. He tries to be selective, choosing partners who can keep up while still making the less skilled look good. He is a gift — a living artifact of a vanishing era. Watching him dance is like watching Fred Astaire. Women who dance with him glow.

As a teacher, he is uncompromising. He spots the slightest flaw. If you try to fake it, he shakes his head, mutters an invective (sometimes in Yiddish), and exaggerates your mistake until you laugh at yourself. It's not unlike psychotherapy — sometimes you must magnify the distortion to help someone see it. A true professional perceives what others miss.

But mastery has a cost. When you develop a refined eye — in dance, music, art, or human behavior — you lose the ability to enjoy the ordinary without judgment. Letting go of criteria is hard. It requires a shift in consciousness.

I often think of Andy Warhol, who seemed to view everything as art — soup cans, Brillo boxes, the mundane. Perhaps he achieved a kind of transcendence, a loosening of the evaluative mind. Maybe he saw divinity in all human creations. I sometimes envy that state.

But I don't want Luigi to accept my dancing as it is. Temporary reassurance is pleasant, but growth requires honesty. I've spent years learning from experts in dance, skiing, golf, tennis, conga drumming, and psychoanalysis. Seven years on the couch, five days a week, with a brilliant analyst. If all my teachers had been Warhols, I might have ended up a Buddhist monk — perhaps a better path, certainly a more peaceful one, like Chauncey Gardner in *Being There*, walking on water.

But that wasn't my path. I remain committed to mastery — or at least the pursuit of it. Complete mastery may elude me, but the joy is in the striving. Life is short. We do what we can to feel we live it well. For me, that means setting goals, committing to them, and taking action.

Addendum: It was skiing, marathon running, and tennis. Now it is golf, writing, and dancing. Who knows what comes next? If something feels vital, purposeful, and worth doing, we can look forward to it with anticipation. Giving it our best shot makes the journey worth the effort.

TRANSITION INTO "YOU AIN'T NOBODY"

After exploring the friendships, passions, and inner freedoms that define late life, the journey naturally turns inward. Beneath the pleasures of mastery and companionship lies a quieter truth — that aging is not only an expansion but a narrowing, a gradual stripping away of illusions, roles, and defenses.

You Ain't Nobody enters here, where identity meets mortality, and where the self is confronted not with who it has become, but with what remains when the scaffolding of life begins to fall away.

YOU AIN'T NOBODY

"When we are no longer able to change a situation, we are challenged to change ourselves." — Viktor Frankl.

Any allusions to ethnic manners of speech have no racially biased implications. They reflect the reality of a specific moment in time central to this essay's theme.

"You ain't nobody, boy, you hear? You ain't nobody at all! You think you somethin'. Looka here, look at you, strutting around thinking you something… You ain't nobody, nobody, nothing at all. You wait; you'll find out!"

He could barely catch his breath, yet he kept shouting, then laughing, then sobbing in a way that felt unhinged and unbearably human. The three of us stood helplessly at his bedside. I was twenty-four, a third-year medical student, and I had never been spoken to like that by a dying man.

His skin was jaundiced. His wrists flapped involuntarily — asterixis. His breath carried the unforgettable sweetness of liver failure — *fetor hepaticus*, the "breath of the dead." It was September 1963, and we were learning medicine on the bodies of poor inner-city people, who had no choice but to let rookies examine them.

His words struck me then, but they strike me harder now, sixty-three years later, as I live with incurable stage-four metastatic prostate cancer.

For twenty years after my 2003 radical prostatectomy at MSKCC, I lived with cautious optimism. Then the fickle finger of fate delivered its curveball. Dormant adenocarcinoma — invisible for years — revealed itself in my eighth left rib, my L4 pedicle, and three subcarinal pulmonary lymph nodes. "Oligometastatic," they called it. Oddly, nothing lit up in the prostate bed. For years, I was told recurrence was unlikely. Perhaps it was micro-metastatic from the start, held in check by a younger immune system. At eighty-plus, all bets are off.

Why write about this? Why not numb myself with Netflix, golf, or backgammon instead of confronting the emotions that accompany the awareness of a shortened life? When we are young or relatively unscarred, we assume — naively — that we will live at least as long as our parents. My father made it to 85. My mother to 101. Watching her die the "perfect death" created a benchmark of confidence.

But confidence is not immunity.

The "doublet" therapy — Orgovyx and Nubeqa — has chemically castrated me. My testosterone dropped from 738 to undetectable in weeks. My PSA, which crept from 0.06 in 2017 to 2.01 in 2022, is now undetectable again. How long I remain sensitive to treatment is unknown. Once I cross into "castration-resistant" territory, the horizon narrows unless a new therapy emerges. I have no actionable mutations for the newly targeted treatments. What I receive is palliative.

Still, gratitude must remain on the front burner. Many friends never made it to 86. Cancer, heart disease, neurodegeneration — the usual suspects. One strong, healthy friend was killed instantly by a texting driver during a morning walk. I now stop at every corner and look both ways twice.

Vulnerability crucifies the ego. That dying man's words echo: "You ain't nobody."

With the Grim Reaper on our tail, we marvel at how the body fights to survive — viruses, bacteria, fungi, cancers — all mutating, hiding, resisting our attempts to suppress them. They outmaneuver us. They persist. Unless we outfox them, they win. Impermanence is not a concept. It is a biological fact.

I've tried to adopt an Eastern approach to dying. Zen, meditation, non-attachment. But belief does not arrive on command. I have no time for an ashram, and no sudden epiphany has swept me into acceptance. I cannot will myself into serenity.

In a moment of curiosity, I typed "You Ain't Nobody" into an AI program. What came back stunned me — a poetic counter-narrative of cosmic belonging, defiance, and worth. It moved me to tears. I wondered whether reading it repeatedly, as the devout recite prayers, might hypnotically ease my fear of dying.

I envy those whose belief systems were imprinted early, whose faith offers comfort now. My religious experience never fully took. God, the afterlife — they always felt as plausible as ghosts or Santa Claus. Yet I still say, "Thank God," "God forbid," "God only knows." Does habitual language reveal hidden belief, or is it cultural hypnosis?

Perhaps trying to pre-solve dying is pointless. Life happens, lessons arrive, and then it ends. What follows is a story we revise endlessly.

It would be comforting to believe "It's all in God's hands," say a prayer, and drift to sleep. The AI's message — "You are everything" — is more appealing than "You ain't nobody," but I can't fully buy it. Not yet. Maybe tomorrow. Maybe never.

In the meantime, I'll welcome what I can, stay close to believers, and hope their faith rubs off. Maybe I'll catch it. Maybe my fear will soften. Maybe the possibility of a quasi-afterlife will feel like a plus.

For now, I live in the tension between "You ain't nobody" and "You are everything," trying to make peace with both.

Addendum: This essay was written more than twenty years after *Reflections on Coming Home*, and it carries the unmistakable voice of a man who has lived long enough to see the arc of his life from a new vantage point. It's a deepening — a late-life reckoning with identity, mortality, and the fragile narratives that sustain us. If the early essays wrestled with becoming, this one wrestles with unbecoming, and with the possibility that both are illusions. It completes the circle.

TRANSITION OUT OF "YOU AIN'T NOBODY" AND INTO THE FINAL CODA

After walking through the raw edge of impermanence — the dissolution of ego, the body's betrayals, the narrowing horizon — the manuscript no longer needs another confrontation. It needs an exhale. *You Ain't Nobody* has taken us as far as reckoning can go. Beyond that point, the argument collapses, philosophy thins, and even courage becomes quieter.

What remains is the human longing beneath all the striving: the desire to be known, to be met, to be understood. When the scaffolding of identity begins to fall away, what we reach for is not mastery or explanation, but connection — the simple recognition that our life was witnessed, that our presence mattered to someone.

The final coda enters here, not to resolve the unresolvable, but to offer a place to land. It does not compete with the emotional force of what came before; it softens it. It opens a small clearing where the reader — and the writer — can sit with the mystery without trying to solve it. After so much stripping away, this is where the mind and heart naturally go: toward spaciousness, toward tenderness, toward the quiet truth that even in the face of impermanence, the need to be understood endures.

BEING UNDERSTOOD — THE ULTIMATE APHRODISIAC

"Only the development of compassion and understanding for others can bring us the tranquility and happiness we all seek." — Dalai Lama XIV.

Few experiences have the power to regulate the human psyche as profoundly as being understood. It is the antidote to loneliness, the corrective to early wounds, the bridge between two separate minds. We long for someone who can track our intentions, perceive our vulnerabilities, and register the emotional logic beneath our words. When that happens, the nervous system shifts; the body softens; the self becomes more coherent. For me, understanding is the precondition for love, trust, and intimacy. It begins with the discipline of attention.

To be understood requires a rare combination of repose, skill, and willingness. This calibrated responsiveness resonates deeply and offers a reprieve from the stark reality of moving through life as separate, distinct, and often lonely beings. We long for the illusion of fusion, a temporary return to the blissful, undifferentiated state we once knew in the womb.

But we live in a turbulent world — internally and externally. Our minds are bombarded by digital noise, responsibilities, and emotional clutter. Focus is hard. Presence is harder.

Who are the people capable of hitting the empathic bull's-eye? Many believe they can, but in truth, most are clueless. Despite good intentions, they lack the intuitive and intellectual skills required. Their inner dialogue contaminates their listening. Their mental clutter impairs concentration. They respond from their own needs rather than the speaker's. And when their efforts fall flat, they externalize the problem rather than look inward.

Several forces interfere with genuine listening. Some people are too egocentric — more invested in impressing than understanding. Others are compulsive rescuers, eager to dispense wisdom rather than sit with another's pain. Some interrupt to restore a sense of mutuality, unable to tolerate the imbalance inherent in deep listening. And some simply take up all the air in the room, oblivious to the listener's fatigue.

When the listener finally reins them in, shame, rejection, and disappointment flood the speaker — especially if childhood wounds are involved.

For many, feeling misunderstood is a lifelong trigger. If parents lacked empathy, patience, or presence, the child internalized a template of emotional neglect. As adults, these individuals react disproportionately to misunderstandings because they reactivate the original wound. They often reenact the same painful dynamics with partners and friends, hoping unconsciously to repair what was broken — and failing repeatedly.

As a psychiatrist, I spent forty years listening to people more deeply than their families ever could. The therapeutic relationship is a one-way street: the patient receives unconditional attention without needing to reciprocate. In the early phase, the therapist becomes an idealized parental figure — perfectly attuned, endlessly patient, unconditionally accepting. Erotic or familial transference emerges. The patient feels understood in a way they never have before. It is intoxicating. It is the ultimate aphrodisiac.

But if therapy is real, the honeymoon ends. Silence enters. Frustration surfaces. Childhood wounds reappear. The therapist becomes the target of displaced anger. And then the work begins. When the patient eventually feels understood in a realistic, grounded way — not idealized, not fantasized — the true aphrodisiac returns. Not the love of the therapist, but the love of the self that emerges through understanding.

For those who never enter therapy, the healing antidote is a loving, compassionate listener — someone capable of offering the corrective emotional experience of being understood. Without that nourishment, why remain in the relationship at all?

Once restored, solitude becomes preferable to the familiar dysfunction of chronic misunderstanding. If we endure being alone long enough, we learn to enjoy our own company. Then we can choose relationships selectively, without settling.

Some argue that settling is necessary because humans are inherently flawed and perfect mutuality is impossible. Perhaps. But the real question is not whether misunderstanding will occur — it will — but how much misunderstanding we can tolerate.

We are complex beings. We never fully understand ourselves, let alone others. Expecting perfect comprehension from an untrained, unanalyzed mortal is unrealistic. Some tolerate misunderstanding easily; others take offense quickly. What determines the difference?

Is it grandiose to expect a long-term friend or partner to know who we are by now? If they don't, why not? Have they not paid attention? Or is something about us — transparent, communicative, expressive — still somehow elusive to them?

How many strikes before we say, "Enough"? Or do we overlook the insensitivities and focus on the positives to avoid living as a soloist?

We want someone capable of giving us the degree of understanding we need — and we want to give it back in kind. True mutuality enhances our capacity to thrive.

We attract what we have become. If we find ourselves stuck in dysfunctional dynamics, it's because we are replaying unresolved issues with someone doing the same. Once we stop participating in that symbiotic dance, healthier connections emerge. Then the dance of love begins — open, exposed, vulnerable, real.

As a final reflection, it is difficult for a psychiatrist to expect reciprocity from someone without similar training or deep personal analysis. The depth of communication, vulnerability, responsibility, and self-understanding cultivated through long-term analysis is a rare gift. Without it, relationships can feel skewed and one-sided.

Analysis is an exclusive club — like medical training, combat, or addiction recovery. You cannot fully understand it unless you've lived it.

My lifelong desire to be understood is inseparable from the forty years I spent understanding others. As the sun sets on the horizon, I, too, long for someone who truly gets who I am and how I came to be. Misunderstanding is intolerable now — not worth the emotional labor required to untangle distortions. Compassion for those who cannot comprehend is one thing; maintaining close friendships with them is another.

Listening to disordered communication feels like hearing music played off key — the shrill scrape of fingernails on a blackboard. Professionally, I reframed it as academic curiosity. Personally, I no longer have the appetite.

If I point out communication distortions to friends, many take umbrage — for insights my patients once paid handsomely to receive. So, I remain silent, focusing on their strengths, deciding whether the friendship is worth keeping. Life is too short to spend my remaining years doing unpaid therapeutic labor.

This essay, like all the others, is an attempt to be heard, acknowledged, appreciated, and understood — a gift to myself and, I hope, to others. Some readers will resonate deeply; others will process information differently. Some believe nirvana lies solely in meditation, minimizing the cognitive work I've described. But meditation has helped me write, listen, and communicate more fluidly. My approach — a mindfulness-based, cognitive-psychodynamic reconstruction — feels like the best of all worlds.

Addendum: As Sinatra sang in 1955, "Love and marriage… go together like a horse and carriage." So do understanding and connection. Without understanding, love falters. With it, everything becomes possible.

TRANSITION OUT AND INTO THE FINAL CODA

After all this searching—for meaning, for connection, for understanding—what remains is not a conclusion but a settling. The final coda doesn't resolve what came before; it simply opens a small, steady space where the reader, and the writer, can rest in what has been uncovered.

THE QUIET OF ENOUGH

Contentment is not a dramatic emotion. It doesn't arrive with fanfare or revelation. It settles in quietly, almost imperceptibly, like a soft light filling a room without asking to be noticed. For much of my life, I mistook that quietness for complacency. I believed that striving was proof of vitality, that ambition was synonymous with meaning, that rest was something earned rather than something allowed.

It took decades — and more than a few humbling lessons — to understand that contentment is not the absence of desire, but the presence of *enough*.

Enough connection. Enough purpose. Enough clarity to know what matters and what doesn't. Enough awareness to recognize the difference between wanting and needing.

Late in life, "enough" becomes less about accumulation and more about perspective. It reveals itself in the ordinary moments — a conversation, a familiar face, a quiet morning, a small pleasure — the moments I once dismissed as background noise. They were never the background. They were the point.

Contentment is not static. It shifts, deepens, contracts, expands. It asks only that we stop long enough to notice what is already here. After a lifetime of striving, resisting, longing, regretting, and reinventing, I find myself returning to something simple: the quiet satisfaction of being alive, of being connected, of being present in whatever time remains.

If there is a final lesson to be learned from all of this, it is that contentment is not something we chase. It is something we allow.

And so, in the time that remains, I choose to stand in the quiet of enough, grateful for the life that brought me here.

REFERENCES

1. Jorge Luis Borges, Twenty Conversations with Borges, Including a Selection of Poems: Interviews by Roberto Alifano, 1981–1983 (1984).
2. Sheldon B. Kopp, If You Meet the Buddha on the Road, Kill Him: The Pilgrimage of Psychotherapy Patients (1982).
3. William Shakespeare, Hamlet, Act 3, Scene 1.
4. Friedrich Nietzsche, Twilight of the Idols (1888), "Maxims and Arrows," aphorism 8.
5. Hsin Hsin Ming: The Book of Nothing, Discourses on the Faith Mind of Sosan.
6. The Beatles, "Let It Be," Let It Be (1970).
7. Winston Churchill, "Success is not final; failure is not fatal…"
8. Thomas Moore, English folk song, Child Ballad No. 167.
9. Oliver Wendell Holmes Sr., The Autocrat at the Breakfast Table (1858).
10. Rabbi Hillel, "If I am not for myself, who will be for me?…"
11. Plato, Apology, 38a.
12. Friedrich Nietzsche, Thus Spoke Zarathustra (1883–1885).
13. Rodney Dangerfield, "I don't get no respect."
14. Ralph Waldo Emerson, "For everything you have missed…"
15. Dylan Thomas, "Do Not Go Gentle into That Good Night," Collected Poems (1952).
16. Frank Loesser, "Praise the Lord and Pass the Ammunition" (1942).
17. Rita Mae Brown, "A life of reaction is a life of slavery…"
18. Rudyard Kipling, Just So Stories (1902), "The Elephant's Child."
19. George Bernard Shaw, "Man is unique in that he has plans…"
20. Voltaire, La Bégueule, "The perfect is the enemy of the good."
21. Helen Keller, "When one door of happiness closes…"
22. Something's Gotta Give (2003), dir. Nancy Meyers.
23. Heraclitus, "Everything flows, and nothing abides."
24. Peggy Lee, "Is That All There Is?" (1969).
25. Kirk Douglas, Champion (1949).
26. Albert Camus, The Myth of Sisyphus (1942).

27. Meister Eckhart (attributed), "If the only prayer you said…"
28. Jean-Baptiste Alphonse Karr, "The more things change…"
29. Zen Koan #18, Buddhist Teaching on Compassion.
30. Peace Pilgrim, "Anything you cannot relinquish…"
31. George Carlin, "A house is just a place to keep your stuff…"
32. Mervyn Stockwood, "A psychiatrist is a man who goes to the Folies-Bergère…"
33. Mignon McLaughlin, "Don't be yourself. Be a little nicer."
34. Chinese Proverb, "Parents who are afraid to put their foot down…"
35. John Powell, "Honest, open communication is the only street…"
36. George Carlin, "Seven Words You Can Never Say on Television" (1972).
37. Ken Keyes Jr., "You are not responsible for the programming…"
38. Ani DiFranco, "If you like it, let it be…"
39. Ben Affleck, "I feel plagued by insecurity."
40. Plato (attributed to John Watson/Ian Maclaren), "Be kind, for everyone you meet…"
41. James Patterson, "What's worse than knowing you want something…"
42. Kenny Rogers, "The Gambler."
43. Oscar Wilde, "Consistency is the last refuge of the unimaginative."
44. Unfaithful (2002), dir. Adrian Lyne.
45. Moonstruck (1987), dir. Norman Jewison.
46. My Dinner with Andre (1981), dir. Louis Malle.
47. E.E. Cummings, "It takes courage to grow up…"
48. François de La Rochefoucauld, "When love becomes labored…"
49. The Bridges of Madison County (1995), dir. Clint Eastwood.
50. Nena and George O'Neill, Open Marriage (1972).
51. Henry David Thoreau, "Every creature is better alive than dead…"
52. Thomas Szasz, M.D.
53. Blaise Pascal, "The heart has its reasons…"
54. Thomas Jefferson, "Do not bite at the bait of pleasure…"
55. Marquise du Deffand, "Women are never stronger…"

56. Confucius (attributed), "The first woman was created from the rib of a man…"
57. Wilt Chamberlain, A View from Above.
58. Deep Throat (1972); Beyond the Green Door (1972); The Opening of Misty Beethoven (1976).
59. Plato's Retreat, NYC (1977–1985).
60. Chippendales (founded 1979).
61. Kay Knudsen, "Love that we cannot have…"
62. Pearl Bailey, "Don't hide from the past…"
63. H.G. Wells, The Time Machine (1895).
64. Voltaire, "Use, do not abuse…"
65. Seigneur de Saint-Évremond, "It becomes a man who is no longer young…"
66. John Heywood (1546), "There is no fool like an old fool."
67. Douglas MacArthur, "You are as young as your faith…"
68. Oscar Wilde, "Everything in the world is about sex except sex…"
69. François de La Rochefoucauld, "We are so accustomed to disguise ourselves…"
70. Jean Racine, "There are no secrets that time does not reveal."
71. Homer, The Odyssey, the Sirens.
72. Sammy Davis Jr., "You always have two choices…"
73. Robert Louis Stevenson, "The sweets come last."
74. Woody Allen, "I'm not afraid of death…"
75. Author Unknown, "To a mother, a son is never a fully grown man…"
76. Sigmund Freud (attributed), "Sometimes a cigar is just a cigar."
77. Friedrich Nietzsche, "To die proudly when it is no longer possible to live proudly…"
78. Washington Irving, "A mother is the truest friend we have…"
79. Author Unknown, "'Tis better to buy a small bouquet…"
80. Marcus Tullius Cicero, "The life of the dead is placed in the memory of the living."
81. T.S. Eliot, "The Love Song of J. Alfred Prufrock."
82. Madeleine L'Engle, "To be alive is to be vulnerable."
83. Douglas Adams, "The thing that cannot possibly go wrong…"
84. Not Fade Away (2012), dir. David Chase.

85. Mahatma Gandhi, "Satisfaction lies in the effort…"
86. Henry David Thoreau, "Simplify, simplify."
87. William Makepeace Thackeray, "A thousand thoughts are lying within a man…"
88. Brian Kessler, "The closest to being in control…"
89. Gene Bedell, Three Steps to Yes.
90. Russ Hodges, "The Giants win the pennant!"
91. Yiddish Proverb, "Man plans, God laughs."
92. John Ed Pearce, "Home is a place you grow up wanting to leave…"
93. Ashley Montagu, Growing Young.
94. Percy Boomer, "If you wish to hide your character…"
95. Mark Twain, "Always do right…"
96. C.S. Lewis, The Four Loves.
97. Henning Bech, on male friendship and anxiety.
98. Alfred Lord Tennyson, "The happiness of a man…"
99. Brian Weiss, Many Lives, Many Masters (1988).
100. Friedrich Nietzsche, "Those who were seen dancing…"
101. Being There (1979), dir. Hal Ashby.
102. Robert Louis Stevenson, "We are all travelers in the wilderness…"
103. Dalai Lama XIV, "Only the development of compassion and understanding…"
104. Superman/Clark Kent, created by Jerry Siegel and Joe Shuster (1938).